M000189543

WHEN **CAMP** **ONANDA** GIVES HER CALL

Camp History on Canandaigua Lake

CAROL TRUESDALE
FOREWORD BY RAY HENRY

THE
History
PRESS

Published by The History Press
Charleston, SC 29403
www.historypress.net

Copyright © 2015 by Carol Truesdale
All rights reserved

First published 2015

Manufactured in the United States

ISBN 978.1.62619.289.8

Library of Congress Control Number: 2015934856

Notice: The information in this book is true and complete to the best of our knowledge. It is offered without guarantee on the part of the author or The History Press. The author and The History Press disclaim all liability in connection with the use of this book.

All rights reserved. No part of this book may be reproduced or transmitted in any form whatsoever without prior written permission from the publisher except in the case of brief quotations embodied in critical articles and reviews.

Contents

Foreword

In 1907, the village of Canandaigua's board of trade (predecessor of the Canandaigua Chamber of Commerce) penned a booklet titled *Canandaigua, Its Advantages, Growth and Beauty* to "call attention to many of Canandaigua's leading features." In that effort, in its introduction, it stated, "In recent years the Village has become more than ever popular as a summer resort, and along the tree embowered and vine clad shores of the loveliest of Western New York lakes has grown up a summer colony which finds in the bracing air, the limpid beauty of the waters and the rugged glory of the hills, a welcome relief from the stifling bounds of encircling walls and glaring pavements."

Through the first few decades of the 1900s, before paved roads and SUVs, before electric lines and Ma Bell, before $3,000-per-foot shoreline prices and before modern affluence, life on Canandaigua Lake was laid-back and simple. Groceries were delivered by boat, as was the mail, especially toward the steeply hilled south end. The steamboats made regular stops at many of the points. Names like Hope Point, Tichenor Point, Menteth Point, Foster's Point, Point Rochester, Seneca Point, Granger Point, Woodville, Cook's Point and Black Point were regular stops for the big, smoke belching steamers. Red Dock, Bay View, Lapham's Point, Davidson's Landing and Main Top also had wooden docks with flagpoles used to signal the need for a steamer. Most sites were either hotels or family cottages without electricity. As with all the Finger Lakes, the roads that accommodated horses and buggies and early autos, such as West Lake Road, were dirt or gravel. Canandaigua's highway superintendant Ira Cribb was the first in Upstate New York to develop and successfully implement the oil and stone application on rural roads. At that point in time, West Lake Road was narrow and twisting and not conducive to any speed. To the residents, it was a dead-end road. Ontario County maps as late as 1920 show West Lake Road as an "improved highway" only from the city limits to Tichenor Point.

Children's laughter echoed from the swing sets and beach picnic tables at the district school on the corner of Butler Road. A great deal of activity could be seen at the riding academy at the Denton farm. Many children and young adults enjoyed hikes and sports at the numerous camps along the west side of the lake, including the natural science camp at Tichenor Point.

The booklet also declared:

> *It is difficult to describe the beauties of the lake itself and of the surrounding country without running the risk of inducing incredulity in the average reader, but the fact remains that many who have had opportunity to view the famous resorts of this and other countries concur in saying that for attractive features Canandaigua Lake is surpassed by few small bodies of water either in this country or abroad...As the traveler proceeds up the lake his eye is regaled with an ever changing vista, showing gradually less and less of the characteristics of the agricultural landscape and merging into a delightful confusion of lofty hillsides covered with the primeval growth and as yet practically unscarred by the implements of industry...There are a number of good resorts along the lake where pleasant rooms and good board may be obtained at a reasonable rate and attractive cottages may also be rented during the summer.*

Canandaigua Lake had long been a summer mecca for many families, dating back to the mid-1800s. In fact, most residents in those times and up to World War II were primarily summer residents, starting as soon as school was out in late June and then packing up and heading home on Labor Day weekend. They came by steamboat, horse and buggy and auto (to the extent that they could navigate the narrow, steep one-lane roadways).

Enter Camp Onanda on the scene. *Onanda* is an Indian word meaning "tall fir" or "pine," a symbol of strength and simplicity. In 1911, William Foster, an early owner of this site, passed away. Later in that year, the Young Women's Christian Association (YWCA) of Rochester, Monroe County, New York, began renting the home and grounds as a place where working adult women could rest and enjoy recreational activities. In 1919, the YWCA purchased the property known as Shale Rock from the W.L. Foster Estate. Over the next several years, many of the buildings that exist there today where constructed, and by the mid-1920s, the YWCA had begun using the camp for junior campers as well as adult women.

The park has a rich history, including its original purpose as the YWCA Leisure Time School (starting in the early twentieth century) and at one time, the site of Camp Good Days and Special Times. A cooperative purchasing effort in 1989 by the Town of Canandaigua; the New York State Department of Parks, Recreation and Historic Preservation; and the Department of Environmental Conservation was successful in an effort to improve recreational opportunities and access for the public. It was opened as such in 1990. Fishing, swimming, family picnics and gatherings have proven popular at this year-round recreation area.

Located on West Lake Road (County Road 16), today's Onanda is an exceptional and unique property about eight miles south of the city of Canandaigua—truly a gem in the middle of the Finger Lakes. Today, it encompasses eighty acres, seven of which are lakeside and house eight cabins, two pavilions and two lodges, and all of which are available to the public. The seventy-three acres of hillside running along Barnes Road contain a two-mile hiking path, three pavilions, seven cabins, winter sledding and overflow parking.

As a lifelong resident of the Canandaigua area and present town of Canandaigua historian, I have hoped, for many years, to have a history of this vital town asset penned by someone who has had an intimate relationship with the camp and shares the desire to bring its history to public awareness. Carol Truesdale, a past counselor at the camp, has used her life experience and time with the YWCA to weave this biological sketch of Onanda.

I have known Carol for several years, and we have shared a love of Canandaigua Lake history. Besides her years with the camp, Carol and her family spent many years summering on the east side of Canandaigua Lake at the cottage they built at the foot of Genundewah (Bare Hill). And she admits, "If I was to seriously consider the experiences that have truly impacted my life, at the very top of such a list would be Canandaigua Lake, followed by travel and teaching."

A 1972 graduate of the State University of New York–Geneseo, Carol taught English, history and reading to classes ranging from first to sixth grade in the Churchville-Chili Central School District of Monroe County, New York, over a twenty-five-year career. She uses her well-honed educational talents to craft an interesting story of the Camp Onanda years.

FOREWORD

As Mark Twain has quipped, "The only difference between fiction and reality is that fiction must be credible." The stories Carol tells of the fun and camaraderie of life at the YWCA camp through the decades will remain with the reader for a long time to come as a very enjoyable biographical sketch.

RAY HENRY
Town of Canandaigua historian

Acknowledgements

Nothing one does in life is truly done alone.

After a few years spent chasing after facts, collecting memories from others and laboring many late nights at the computer, this history of Camp Onanda finally fell into shape. Even though I knew that it was truly impossible to convey the impact this camp has had on so many lives, as the final period was placed, I was instantly grateful for all the support and encouragement that I had received.

I first thought of my parents, my first and best teachers. Their guiding words and values have carried me well through life and this endeavor. Laughter came in when I thought of my good friend Sally and Aunt Merlene, who kindly endured my voiced frustrations and doubts that this would be completed. They were my constant cheerleaders.

It was Mr. Ray Henry, town of Canandaigua historian, who initially suggested this project and was ever ready to fill in a gap for me, ponder a wonder with me or offer up a suggested resource. His patience and eagerness to uncover this history fairly and accurately made him a rare mentor. Thanks, RPM.

Dennis Brewer, director of parks and recreation for the Town of Canandaigua, has been involved with Onanda Park practically since the land was acquired from the Rochester YWCA. His sharing of the park's development was greatly appreciated.

No, this was not done alone. Lea Kemp of the Schuyler C. Townson Research Library at the Rochester Museum and Science Center not only

Onanda staff, 1970. *Courtesy of Nancy Showalter-Clark.*

An Onanda reunion gathering. *Author's collection.*

convinced me that I could do this but also found just the right materials and offered wonderful suggestions as I began. The Albert P. Stone Photo Collection is what started our friendship. Lori Birrell, historical manuscripts librarian at the University of Rochester Library of Rare Books and Special Collections, was always there to pull whatever I requested from the YWCA Collection, and requests were many. Whitney Landis and Katie Stitely of The History Press are saints. Their patience and care to every detail of this book were incredible. I simply cannot adequately thank these awesome women.

So many people stepped up. Mr. Ross Anderson shared personal photos of the rental cottages of Onanda's earliest years and his adventures as a raider of Camp Onanda. Helen Smith, the great-granddaughter of Marian Crouch, provided me with a deeper connection to her great-grandmother. Michael Otto and Wendy Ulatowski of the Apple store rescued me from my lack of computer skills. Without Mike's help, I honestly don't know how any printable document would have been completed. Wendy, an incredible computer detective, found my lost manuscript. The list could go on for pages. Just know that I'm fully aware that this story was accomplished because so many people stepped up to help and enriched the telling.

Then, too, when anyone from Camp Onanda calls out to Onanda folks, they answer. When I called out, without pause or hesitation, many of the campers and staff shared memories, letters home, personal camp photos and their excitement that Onanda's history would be told. Thank you all, with special thanks to Barb, Dana, Perk, Kammy, Nancy and Candi, who saved so many pictures and shared so much of their personal connection with Onanda. Thank you, Sarah and Cat, for your constant enthusiasm and for keeping me focused on the depth of the positive impact that Camp Onanda had on so many of us. You, the campers and staff of Camp Onanda, were not just the motivation for this story. You are the story.

Introduction

Connecting with Canandaigua Lake

From the age of five, I spent almost every weekend from April through October on Canandaigua Lake. My dad had purchased land along the cliffs on the east side of this glacial wonder of crystal-clear water and built a cottage on its shore nearly at the base of Bare Hill.

It was here, with my dad, that I learned of worms and lures, how to untangle fishing line and how to net a caught fish. It was here that I learned to swim and sail, respecting the power of water, its dangers and joys. It was here that I learned from my mother how to make wonderful meals without all the conveniences of our Rochester home. It was here that I learned of nature with my older, more adventuresome brother. We climbed up steep ravines and hiked through pathless woods. We found fossils, encountered animals and learned what poison ivy was about. Yes, it was here on Canandaigua Lake that I learned the lessons that thoroughly enriched my life.

Canandaigua Lake is the fourth largest of the Finger Lakes of New York State. It's nestled near the western end of the eleven lakes that stretch across the western midsection of the state, from Syracuse to Rochester. Almost like a good fish story, some locals will claim that Canandaigua Lake is eighteen miles long, while it's truly about 16.16 miles long. West River flows into Canandaigua Lake at its southern foot, and the city of Canandaigua graces its northern end. The surface of the lake is 689 feet above sea level and reaches to a depth of 227 feet. The thirty-six miles of coveted shoreline is shared by Ontario and Yates Counties, though the larger portion falls in Ontario County, as does the city of Canandaigua. Squaw Island, at the

Canandaigua Lake. *Author's collection.*

north end, is the smallest fish and wildlife management area in the entire state of New York and is one of only two islands found among the eleven Finger Lakes.

It is no wonder that the Seneca Indians claimed their birth from Bare Hill, on the east side of the lake, and called this land the "Chosen Spot." While somewhat appalling, it isn't all that surprising that the earliest Europeans saw the potential of this land and took it for their own.

Today, Canandaigua Lake's shoreline is dotted with older cottages and elegant homes. It has become a summer destination for those with grand boats, fishing boats, sailboats, canoes and kayaks. Its beauty has endured many changes but will remain the "Chosen Spot" forever.

It was by accident, perhaps, that I was connected with the YWCA's Camp Onanda on the western shore of Canandaigua Lake. By accident or fate, for three summers in the late 1960s, I experienced Camp Onanda as a waterfront counselor. For nine weeks each of those summers, I shared my sailing and swimming skills, earning a whopping $50 at the end of my first summer and $125 my last summer. What I came away with in terms of life experiences and memories was priceless. Camp Onanda, like our family cottage across the lake, has been with me my entire life. Its impact on my teaching, appreciation of nature, friendships, laughter and pranks is unquestionable. Camp Onanda remains one of the most treasured stops on my life journey.

From 1906 through 1989, Camp Onanda called from the west side of Canandaigua Lake and campers answered. Girls came from all parts of New York State and even farther away to experience the truly unique adventure of summer camp. Even before the YWCA of Rochester purchased the land that would become Onanda, its history was full, and today, it's history continues as Onanda Park. Though smaller than the point of a fine needle in the scope of the world, this wee speck of land has touched many lives, and its history merits telling.

Alas, history, be it of a person, family, land or event, is as slanted, detailed or colorful as its writer and his or her research. It's a hard task to weave a truly unbiased yet interesting and informative account of happenings one did not experience. Then, too, relating events one had a part in is challenging. First person memories get foggy. Written accounts are not always complete. Finding the facts is not easy, especially when fond, emotional experiences are the basis. Thus, with heart-felt and sincere research, the history of a small parcel of land and its people is here briefly presented.

Please remember, this is not my story but rather the story of tens of thousands who have walked this parcel of land for hundreds of years. Come along and share a brief peek at the land and people who made this a very special place for so many. You'll need good walking shoes, a sleeping bag, a jacket, a sweatshirt and clothes for all sorts of weather. No radios, iPods, iPads or any other *i* devices are allowed. If you must bring your cellphone, please set it to vibrate. Here we go! Welcome to Onanda!

Before Onanda

BEGINNING AT THE BEGINNING

Creation

No, we won't begin with the creation of the universe but rather the creation of the Finger Lakes of New York State.

It's nearly impossible to imagine, but the Finger Lakes area began to take shape about 550 million years ago. Back then, the area around Canandaigua was nearly a featureless plain. Except for part of the Adirondack Mountains, geologists believe that all of New York was likely just a rolling plain with a scattering of small hills and only slightly above sea level.

You're going to have to put on your winter attire. One million years ago, things abruptly changed. This was change that came in the form of glaciers—yes, the ice age.

Geologists have determined that not one but two mighty glaciers crushed their way over New York State all the way to Williamsport, Pennsylvania. The power of moving a giant 2,500-foot-thick piece of ice over central New York dramatically changed that rolling plain of pre-glacial days. Boulders were displaced; plant life crushed and moved; and the land was simply ravished.

As the ice receded and melted, the deep gashes in the land filled with water. Voila! The Finger Lakes were born.

That process of heavy, moving ice transformed the land's surface and rocks. Having scraped away soils and plants and gouged valleys and troughs, the glacier left behind polished bedrock. The ice even left some deposits of rock that are not common to the area.

All of the Finger Lakes now drain northward, but before the final glacial action, the Finger Lakes from Seneca Lake west (Keuka, Canandaigua, Honeoye, Canadice, Hemlock and Conesus Lakes) drained in the same direction as the Mississippi River. This reversal to a northern drain makes the Finger Lakes a bit of an oddity.

Today, Canandaigua Lake's shoreline is covered in nicely weathered shale. Ravines of all sizes drain from the higher land around it into the lake. The larger ravines make for wonderful hiking and photo opportunities. The layered shale of the towering cliff areas shift and slide easily toward the lake below and is sharp enough to cut hands and feet. Boulders abound as well, all reminders of the long-ago ice age.

Should you have the opportunity to hike up the glen at Onanda Park in the twenty-first century and lose your footing on the sharp and shifting shale or skip a smooth, weathered piece of shale from the waterfront across the lake's surface, remember that glaciers and the constant flow of water provided all that.

THE BIRTH OF A PEOPLE

The Seneca and Their Chosen Place

One cannot write of Onanda or Canandaigua without paying homage to the first people who lived there. Take your jacket off now and settle into a comfortable chair. Better yet, build a cozy fire to add some atmosphere as we learn of the birth of the Haudenosaunee, the People of the Long House and, more specifically, the Seneca Nation people.

The exact date of the birth of the Seneca people is not known. Current and ongoing studies of a site near the town of Canandaigua offices indicate that native peoples had lived in this area far longer than first thought. What is definitely known is that their impact on Canandaigua and the surrounding land is permanent. Through oral history passed among this people and efforts made by others to preserve their history, we are afforded a glimpse of the first known humans to live and prosper for centuries in this wonderful place, the "Chosen Spot."

We know for sure that the Seneca Nation was the largest of the five original tribes to form the Iroquois Confederacy over five hundred years ago. The Seneca were composed of eight clans: Turtle, Bear, Wolf, Beaver, Snipe, Heron, Deer and Hawk. These clans lived off the land approximately from Canandaigua Lake west to the Genesee River, north to Lake Ontario and south into Pennsylvania. They may have hunted well west of the Genesee River, as far as Ohio, if necessary. Because of the location of the Seneca clans in the Iroquois Confederacy, they were known as the "Keepers of the Western Door." The Seneca composed half the fighting force of the Iroquois and were the first to defend the confederacy when it was threatened.

Though fearless and strong, the Seneca were first farmers and hunters. The "three sisters"—squash, maize (corn) and climbing beans—were their staples. Deer, rabbit, fish, beaver, raccoon and many other animals provided meat, utensils and furs. Because the Iroquois often settled near and around water, like Canandaigua Lake, they built canoes to more easily get to and from hunting areas. The Seneca people most often built their canoes at lengths of thirty feet, with the ability to hold up to eighteen passengers. These canoes easily carried large amounts of deer and game when returning from a hunting trip as well as plants and building materials. If it were needed by war parties, the Seneca could build a canoe in one day.

While the Seneca worked hard and provided well, they also enjoyed leisure activities. Seneca children surely were no different from children today. Girls had their dolls and learned to bead, sew and identify helpful plants. Boys, of course, had their bows and arrows, wrestled and emulated the powerful men of their village. Even the adults made time for play—sport, if you will. Young people today can thank the Iroquois for their game of lacrosse. That's right, the Seneca men were avid competitors. One game of their style of lacrosse could last for days and cover miles, going from one village to another.

Alas, games of lacrosse would become less frequent as European explorers found their way into the Finger Lakes region of New York. The Seneca's first encounters with explorers were brief, almost uneventful. When Jacques-René de Brisay de Denonville destroyed a Seneca village (near the modern city of Canandaigua) in July 1687, the Seneca became keenly aware that their land and way of life were in jeopardy.

Initially, the Seneca didn't fight with these pale-skinned people. They were more curious than reactive and would hide nearby where they could simply observe the strangers. Often, the first explorers destroyed the Seneca's homes and food supplies.

Right off the bat, the Seneca men recognized the aggressive nature of the new people and the need to protect their women and children. Thus, we have the story of Squaw Island at the north end of Canandaigua Lake.

In 1779, during the Revolutionary War, when General Sullivan invaded the area, the Seneca women and children found safety on this island. It was much larger then and provided an ideal hiding place. As each invasive group of Europeans came into the area, the squaws and children would be secreted to the island until the invaders moved on. Squaw Island was, for the Seneca people, a place of refuge. Today, Squaw Island is the smallest fish and wildlife management area in New York State.

Though the Seneca people gradually moved away from their place of origin as the Europeans kept coming, their names remain attached to lakes, rivers and towns, as well they should, for it was the Seneca people who cared for this land that we enjoy and now claim as our own. Ontario, Genesee, Keuka, Canoga and even Onanda are reminders that this land was once part of the Iroquois Nation.

If you crave more information about the Iroquois and Seneca, a wealth of firsthand information can be found in Lewis H. Morgan's book *League of the Ho-dé-No-Sau-Nee or Iroquois*. Morgan was the first non-Seneca historian to attempt to put the history, laws, legends and language of the Iroquois to paper. He lived among these people, walked where they walked, deciphered the native tongue and listened. This book was first published in 1851.

Arch Merrill, a prolific writer of local and New York history, wrote *The Land of the Senecas*. In this book, he shared a Seneca legend that is known to almost every resident of Canandaigua and every girl who attended Camp Onanda. It is here shared for you to enjoy and pass along.

The Legend of Bare Hill: The Birth of the Seneca People

Long ago, the Creator caused the earth to open and out of the side of a great hill near a long and lovely lake the ancestors of the Seneca Nation came into being.

For a time, they lived in peace. Then a boy found a little snake in the woods. It was an unusual reptile in that it had two heads. The boy took the snake home, made a pet of it and fed the choicest meat into its twin mouths.

The serpent grew to prodigious size, and its appetite grew with it. Soon its young master could not find enough game to satisfy its hunger. The People of the Great Hill came to fear it as a monster.

Finally, the great snake, in his desperate hunger, encircled the hill and barred the gates with his open jaws so that no one could escape. The people

Bare Hill. *Author's collection.*

grew hungry and tried to get away. One by one, the monster ate them. At last, only a young warrior and his sister remained of all the People of the Hill.

One night the youth had a vision. If he would fletch his arrows with his sister's hair, they would possess a fatal charm over the monster. He followed his dream and shot his magic arrows straight into the great red jaws of the enemy of his People. The reptile was mortally wounded, and in his death agony, he writhed his way down the hill, tearing down trees and flailing the earth until he finally slid into the lake and was seen no more.

As the great snake rolled down the hill, he disgorged the skulls of the Senecas he had devoured.

In the area have been found rounded stones divided into geometric patterns and weirdly resembling human skulls. And to this day nothing has ever grown in the path of the serpent down that hillside.

Again, if you have a chance to skip the glacial shale from the shore of Onanda Park, you can't miss Bare Hill sloping down to the lake's edge. Even today, it's not hard to imagine a group of Seneca men paddling across the lake toward you, bows and tools in tow, heading for their hunting grounds. Hopefully, all of us who call the United States of America our home will remember that this land was well cared for by its true native people, and we should strive to treat it with the same respect and awe.

21

EUROPEANS ARRIVE

Native Americans held no deed to the land they lived on. It wasn't in their nature to claim that they owned the land. They believed they were born of the land and were responsible to it. The Europeans held different beliefs and that meant deeds and proof of ownership.

Once European fur traders and land-hungry explorers began settling along the eastern coast of North America, they kept moving, inching their way westward. Samuel de Champlain touched the edge of Iroquois country in his 1615 exploration. Robert de La Salle, in 1669, actually "visited" a principal Seneca village about twenty miles south of Irondequoit Bay. A few French priests, determined to convert the Iroquois, came in spurts and lived within a clan or two. The arrival of Marquis de Denonville in 1687 was the start of determined aggression by the Europeans toward the Seneca. Denonville was determined to put the Seneca in their place for "inhospitable treatment of French traders." The first documented battle erupted in the hills surrounding current day Victor, New York. Even with the consistent arrival of small bands of Europeans, the Seneca were the undisputed residents of western New York for the three hundred years following Columbus's known voyages.

Europeans not only kept coming but also were staying. More colonies were established and continued to inch into Iroquois country. By the time of the American Revolution, some trading and loosely made pacts had been established between the colonists and Iroquois. Once the permanence of the colonists was realized, the Iroquois Nation was conflicted. Some Iroquois fought with the colonists for their freedom, but others wanted them gone and fought against them.

The most severe action taken against the Six Nations came in 1779. John Sullivan, an American Revolutionary general, led a campaign against Loyalists and the four Iroquois Nations who sided with the British. Loyalists lost their homes and land, and the strength of the Iroquois Confederacy was broken when Sullivan defeated them in the Battle of Newtown.

The victory of the New World colonies from European control came in 1783 with the signing of the Treaty of Paris. Now, the development of the western New York wilderness could proceed. Massachusetts and New York both staked claim to this western wilderness. This land represented a means for both parties to pay their Revolutionary War soldiers for their service and expand their territories. In 1786, the Treaty of Hartford set the compromise. This treaty gave sovereignty over the land to New York, but Massachusetts would have the "pre-emptive" right to obtain titles to the land from the Indians and then sell it.

Massachusetts almost instantly sold its right to the six million acres of land to Oliver Phelps and Nathaniel Gorham for a purchase price of $1 million.

Following some major setbacks, in 1788, Oliver Phelps acquired the rights to a large amount of land from the Iroquois while Gorham, the gentleman politician and a signer of the Declaration of Independence, stayed put in Boston to deal with the commonwealth of Massachusetts. Phelps chose the northern end of Canandaigua Lake to build his land office.

Taking its name from the lake, the village of Canandaigua would continue to grow and prosper into the city of Canandaigua. Oliver Phelps would have his hand on every aspect of this community's beginnings from how the streets would flow to stimulating commerce. He envisioned a complete, self-reliant and stimulating community, and in that, he was highly successful. To attract others to what surely must have seemed a wilderness, he wanted the comforts and civility of the already well-established costal Northeast to be apparent in western New York State.

In 1790, the deputy marshal of the State of New York reported that there were eighteen families, seventy-eight men, twenty women and one slave residing in the village of Canandaigua. Just five years later, the village was described as having sixty "elegant" homes, two inns and several shops. Land outside the village was sold at three dollars an acre and within the village for fifteen dollars.

One of Oliver Phelps's finer endeavors was the establishment of the Canandaigua Academy. With a number of prominent residents of Canandaigua, he set out to establish an academy or seminary of learning in Ontario County.

In January 1791, Oliver Phelps donated a tract of land, three thousand acres on the west side of the lake, to aid in establishing and maintaining the educational institution that would become Canandaigua Academy. All money taken in sales of the land went directly to the school. (Originally established as a private boys' school, it became a public school in 1900, keeping its name and still providing for education of Canandaigua's young minds to this day.)

The Academy Tract, as it was named, had its first settlement by 1810. About one hundred years later, Camp Onanda would rise from a small, northern lakefront point of this tract of land.

History's Challenges

What Is it? Sell's Point, Bell's Point, Park-Hurst Point, Point Rochester, Pierson Point, Sheffield Point, Foster's Point or Rochester Point?

This is where history gets fun and frustrating. Now we're going to take a look at that small point of the Academy Tract, merely a few acres of lakefront that eventually became Camp Onanda. Both Mother Nature and man have a way of making changes that confuse historians. Mother Nature's changes usually alter the shape of the land and flow of water while the changes that man makes are usually changes of names and general errors in those names.

It was customary in the 1800s, especially in rural areas, to name a road or dominant feature after the surname of the person owning the largest portion of nearby land or after where the road would take you. Prior to states and the federal government taking responsibility for maintaining roads, the name of a road might change if the land around it was sold to a new family. For instance, if a road was named Smith Road, it might be because the Smith family owned a huge farm there. However, it might change to Jones Road after the Jones family purchased the land from the Smiths. Thus, a map made while the Smiths owned the land would show Smith Road; a map made after the Smiths sold their land would show the same road as Jones Road. Now you have some folks always referring to that road as Smith Road and others calling it by its new name, Jones Road. Confusing? You bet! This is exactly the kind of confusion that can be traced to the point from which Camp Onanda would rise.

In the *1859 Atlas of Ontario County*, the point that would become part of Camp Onanda's waterfront is named Sell's Point. This is odd because the Bell family home is identified on that point. Furthermore, the Bell family can be traced to deeds. Would the Bell family truly call their point Sell's Point, or was this simply an error by the mapmaker? The *1874 Atlas of Ontario County* clearly shows the same point as Bell's Point. Whatever the answer to the Sell's or Bell's Point question, this demonstrates the sorts of challenges research presents. As the Academy Tract developed, this point changed names many, many times.

Before this point of land would draw young girls to Camp Onanda, it welcomed visitors to a dance floor in the glen, and twice a hotel was attempted. The first hotel was the Park-Hurst, so the point took the hotel's name. This hotel failed to prosper, but a second attempt was made and was called the Rochester. The point was renamed Point Rochester to erase the first failure. This same point was also named Pierson Point and Sheffield Point at different times. Once the William L. Foster family acquired the land on the north side of the point from their uncle, Harvey C. Foster, it became Foster Point on some maps and Shale Rock on the steamboat map of stops. It is impossible to pin down and verify this point's complete history, but we do know that this point was never named Onanda Point and today is called Rochester Point.

Whatever maps you explore or books of history you read, this special point, about eight miles down the west side of the lake from the city of Canandaigua, was formed by glaciers, used by the Seneca Indians, purchased by Phelps and Gorham, settled by families, became YWCA Camp Onanda and today is Onanda Park.

THE YWCA TAKES A STAND FOR WOMEN AND FINDS A POINT

In 1883, just two decades from the War of the Rebellion, as it was still referred to then, eleven forward-thinking Rochester women became keenly aware of the need for housing for the young women who came to work in the city's industry. Those eleven women, with the assistance of supportive and enlightened men, founded the Young Women's Association (YWA) and opened a small boardinghouse in the city of Rochester.

It must be noted that women at this time could not vote, purchase land, build buildings or do many of the things we take for granted today. Many women were working long hours for little pay in garment and other industries throughout the country. The single workingwomen in Rochester were a vital asset to the economy, yet they faced incredible challenges with little support.

The "Rochester Eleven" who initially met in the parlor of First Baptist Church were not among those struggling workingwomen but rather were women of means. They were truly amazing in that they not only were aware of women's needs throughout the country but also would find ways to raise money and form an organization that would help, educate and protect Rochester's female working force. Their primary objective was "to promote the temporal, social, mental, moral and religious welfare of young women, especially such as are dependent on their own exertions for support."

One of the Rochester Eleven was Marian Elizabeth (McLeod) Crouch. To this day, the Crouch name is attached to Onanda.

Marian Crouch (always referred to as Mrs. Frank P. Crouch in newspaper articles and YWCA minutes, as was customary in the era) was well aware of the struggles women faced. Born in 1854 in a log cabin in Henrietta, Monroe County, New York, Marian and her sister, Annette, were left fatherless at the ages of nine and five. Duncan McLeod, Marian's father, was a casualty of the Battle of Gettysburg.

The McLeod women were strong. Marian's mother, now a widow, packed up her girls, moved to Rochester to be near their Ellis family and became a schoolteacher. Surely this life-changing experience made Marian a champion for women. Marian McLeod Crouch knew firsthand of the struggles women faced when on their own. She would be instrumental in the formation of the YWA and a powerful leader within the association for more than forty years. In 1903, Marian became the first chairman of chapters and would remain in that role until 1928.

By 1888, funds had been raised by the Rochester YWA to build a gymnasium that included the first public swimming pool and additional housing for women. It should not be surprising that Susan B. Anthony spoke at its dedication. Now, a young, single woman could rent a room for one dollar a week and meals could be purchased on site for eleven cents.

In 1894, the YWA of Rochester aligned with the worldwide YWCA. This merger assured the continuation of housing and programs begun a decade earlier. Marian Crouch was still at the helm of the chapters and striving for even more programs and opportunities for the women housed and guided by the YWCA.

The boarders at the YWCA were single, often from rural homes or foreign countries. They ranged in age from seventeen to late twenties and had jobs. Many held jobs in the garment industry, such as at Rochester's Hickey-Freeman Company. Others were sales clerks, working on lines at Eastman Kodak, Bausch & Lomb and smaller companies. Most boarders did not have a high school education, but some teachers boarded at the YWCA.

The YWCA of Rochester did not merely provide safe housing. It provided classes in arithmetic, English and health. It provided for safe social gatherings, too, and promoted community service from its residents and members. Seeing a need for a place for "rest, recreation and healthful outdoor living during the summer months," the YWCA started purchasing and renting vacation houses for use by its boarders. The earliest mention of a vacation house appears in the 1899 YWCA records. Forest Lawn, on Lake Ontario, was rent free and could accommodate twelve employed young women. In 1900, a rental vacation house on Irondequoit Bay was added to the list. Then, there it was! In 1906, a rented vacation house at Point Rochester on Canandaigua Lake appears in the records. This, of course, is the very beginning of Camp Onanda.

2
Camp Onanda's Birth

CAMP ONANDA IN THE RENTAL YEARS

1900s

As the twentieth century arrived, Kodak introduced its Brownie Cameras for one dollar, Ford introduced the Model T and electric washing machines were available for the first time. President McKinley and Japan's Prince Ito were assassinated. Plastic was invented, the first flight at Kitty Hawk was attempted, and the New York City subway opened. The first silent movie, *The Great Train Robbery*, was released, and the teddy bear began its history as a beloved companion for children. Baseball's first World Series was played, and far from the United States, Finland became the first European country to give women the right to vote. It was apparent that change was in the air, and the young workingwomen associated with the YWCA of Rochester were well aware that they were a large part of this change.

In the early years of the twentieth century, it was nearly impossible to imagine Camp Onanda as a vacation destination for anyone. In 1906, when the YWCA first started renting homes on the west shore of Canandaigua Lake, the technology we enjoy today was nonexistent: phones were a luxury, and mail moved slowly. This was a much quieter time, a time without television or transistor radios. Many remote areas didn't always have electrical power. Many rural roads were not paved or even designated on all maps.

Simply getting to camp required a lot of effort and planning. Very few people had cars, and those who did would find the road down the west side of Canandaigua Lake challenging at best. The workingwoman housed at the YWCA in Rochester did *not* own cars. They either walked to work or took trolleys in Rochester. Getting to Canandaigua Lake, nearly forty miles away, must have seemed impossible, but get there they did. The gals from Rochester had to take a special trolley from downtown Rochester to the pier at the north end of Canandaigua Lake. Likely from stops along the way at Pittsford, Fishers and Victor, this leg of their journey could have taken as long as two and a half hours. Once at the pier in Canandaigua, they would purchase a ferry ticket for the eight-mile steamboat ride to camp. Depending on the other passenger's destinations, the amount of mail and other deliveries onboard, the steamboat may have made a few stops before dropping the girls off at stop twenty-four, Shale Rock, on Foster's Point.

The Nest. *Courtesy of Ross Anderson.*

At this time, the YWCA rented two cottages on the southern curve of Foster's Point. The girls quickly dubbed one of the rentals the "Nest" and the other the "Big House" or the "Willows."

The Nest survived until the flood of 1972 when it was taken down and a new home built on the site by Ross Anderson. The Ross family summered at the Nest and enjoys this location today. The Willows remains right where it was, though it's been remodeled almost beyond recognition and is currently owned by the Cleary family.

Fireplaces and, perhaps, some kerosene heaters provided indoor heat on cold summer mornings and nippy nights in 1906. The YWCA women escaped the summer's heat by sitting in the shade or taking a dip in the lake. While electricity was commonplace in the cities, it had not reached the west shore of Canandaigua and would not until June 1925. Prior to this, batteries were used to light rural homes.

The records of the Rochester YWCA showed that their effort to provide vacation houses was appreciated. The workingwomen eagerly headed to Canandaigua. These women ranged in age from eighteen to twenty-five. Some grew up on farms, others in cities. All were now working to support

The Willows, also known as the Big House. *Courtesy of Ross Anderson.*

parents or themselves and living away from home and family. A chance to take a reasonably inexpensive vacation with other gals boarding at Rochester's YWCA facilities was a rare treat.

According to Lela Smith, who was in charge of Onanda in the summer of 1909, the camp capacity was thirty-eight, but according to Lela, "The girls were willing to be crowded if only allowed to come." And pack in they did. To ease cramped quarters on warm nights at the Nest, some girls pulled their cots onto the second-level porch and slept "nearly under the stars."

For the single workingwomen living in Rochester, Camp Onanda was a wonderful adventure that couldn't be missed. They were served three meals a day and provided with a reasonable bed that included sheets, a blanket and a pillow. There were options for classes in nature and all sorts of activities not afforded in the city. What more could they want?

The vacationing women could get a packed lunch to take on a hike up the glen. They could fish, read a book or simply bath in the sun. They knitted items for the Red Cross and made blankets from scraps to send to those in need in northern France. Even while enjoying outdoor activities, the gals were also involved with giving back to the community and world.

A stay at Camp Onanda would include at least one steamboat ride around the lake. Girls who felt comfortable on the water might row off with some friends to explore the nearby area. There was always an activity or adventure awaiting, and the Onanda gals welcomed each and every one.

Ruth Jennings, the recreation leader and swimming teacher during some of the rental years, was excited to report that in 1910, "at least twenty-five girls had learned to swim who could not even float when they came to camp."

Evenings were rarely quiet. There might be a dance where "half the girls dressed as boys," the porch decorated with Japanese lanterns and refreshments served. Often the camp's neighbors were invited to an evening of singing and skits (then referred to as stunt nights) with the girls. Weather permitting, once a week, the girls enjoyed a beach supper, and every night, a campfire was a highlight that included special snacks, singing and storytelling.

The YWCA's treasury report for 1909 claimed that the vacation houses were being used and financially holding their own. The two homes on Canandaigua were rented for $359 for the summer. In order to keep the cost of attending camp down, food and laundry service were purchased from local farmers and women. The gals using the camp held baked food sales, sold thrift tickets and did all they could to raise funds for maintaining the camp. After all, the goal of the vacation houses was to give these YWCA's boarders an affordable and safe place to get away from the daily grind.

VACATION HOUSE
Season of 1909
RECEIPTS

	Canandaigua	Sea Breeze	Total
Balance in Bank	$ 35.02		$ 35.02
Donation	1.00	$ 16.72	17.72
Board (Including $25.55 Girls' Vacation Fund)	1,051.50	206.55	1,258.05
Y. W. C. A. (including Balance $.45)	468.10	14.12	482.22
	$1,555.62	$237.39	$1,793.01

DISBURSEMENTS

	Canandaigua	Sea Breeze	Total
Rent	$359.00		$359.00
Labor	339.10	$ 75.65	414.75
Food	564.34	105.02	669.36
House Expense	155.74	17.34	173.08
Laundry	19.37	4.33	23.70
Freight and Carting	45.61	19.00	64.61
Fuel	24.00	3.75	27.75
Office (Postage, Reg. Cards, Dodgers, Rent of Library Books, Telephone	23.21	4.75	27.96
Ice	21.45	5.75	27.20
Car Fare	3.80	1.80	5.60
	$1,555.62	$237.39	$1,793.01

The YWCA 1909 treasury report. *Courtesy of the University of Rochester.*

By 1913, Camp Onanda was well organized and well known; a stay there was in high demand.

In order to secure funds and have its summer homes used, the YWCA did a good job publicizing. The local newspapers often ran articles about the two vacation homes, and in 1913, when Onanda was still a rental property, one such article provided a glimpse of Camp Onanda.

On August 5, 1913, a lengthy article titled "Girls Enjoy Life at YWCA Outing Home—Camp Onanda Affords Inexpensive Vacation—Permanent Summer Home a Necessity" appeared in a Rochester paper.

While the YWCA never referred to its rental properties as "outing homes" but rather vacation houses, the author of this article (not named) presented a vivid picture of life at Camp Onanda in 1913.

Onanda is described as being located "in a cove, where the water is always quiet enough for rowing or canoeing and where excellent opportunity is offered for bathing." That's right, there were no showers or hot water at Camp Onanda's vacation houses so swimming, bathing and washing clothes were all done in the lake.

Remember, this is a lake carved out by two glaciers. Its depth reaches over 275 feet, and the "cove" described is deep enough for a steamboat to dock.

In the warmest of summers, the water temperature might reach to sixty-eight degrees. If one were to bath early in the morning when the air had a nippy edge to it, it had to be a quick washing.

The two buildings in use were described as well. "There are two cottages, the 'Big' Cottage and the 'Nest.'" The Big Cottage (also referred to as the Willows) was where meals were taken. It also provided a few sleeping rooms on the second floor.

The Nest had to be the most fun. This was the primary sleeping quarters, but it also had a large living room with a piano and fireplace where, according to the article, "vesper services on Sundays and parties and entertainments during the week were held." Upstairs in the Nest were sleeping rooms and a large, screened-in sleeping porch. The sleeping porch was preferred.

The day started at 7:00 a.m. Breakfast was at 7:30 a.m., after which hymns were sung. Then it was off to calisthenics. Some free time followed this for hiking, reading, playing tennis or baseball or taking a swim. By 10:00 a.m., classes in swimming, art, writing, dance, crafts and nature were started. Dinner was served at 12:30 p.m., followed by a class or group outreach project. The afternoon might include a hike, sketching, writing a letter or simply resting on the shore or in a shaded area. At 3:00 p.m., there was a free swim and a boating hour for those interested. At 6:00 p.m., supper was served.

Whatever activities were selected, all the girls were required to be on the grounds at 8:30 p.m. This is when they would gather in the Nest and entertain themselves around the fireplace. At 10:00 p.m., the evening activities ended, and any visitors were ushered out of camp. By 10:30 p.m., it was all lights out.

The leadership of the camp changed throughout the summer because a designated full-time director had not yet been established. About every two or three weeks, the leadership changed as different groups arrived, but the daily schedule remained the same.

In all the written histories of Camp Onanda generated by the YWCA of Rochester, Mary Adaline Moulthrop is given credit for naming the camp. According to these histories, Mary had gotten the name "Onanda" from some Seneca Indians. It is also consistently written that Mary Moulthrop was the leader of the camp during the rental years at Rochester Point and well into the first years that the YWCA owned the land next door. Mary's name pops into camp committee records and association committee records from the rental years through the early 1930s, but who was she and what drew her to be involved?

Mary Moulthrop was the second child of Samuel Parker Moulthrop and Mary (Raymond) Moulthrop and a graduate of the University of

Rochester. Mary's father, fondly called "Colonel" Moulthrop, was such an innovative and successful school principal that his name was more familiar to Rochesterians than that of George Eastman, the founder of the Eastman Kodak company. Thus, while it was rare at this time for a woman to attend a university, it's clear that Mary's father was instrumental in seeing her through an extended education. It seems fair, too, to say that Mary was a "daddy's girl." Mary never married but worked over twenty-five years for the YWCA. Highly interested in genealogy, she found time to publish a history of her family, including its *Mayflower* arrival.

Mary's father was extremely interested in the Native American population and its history. The Colonel had firsthand contact with Seneca Indians and even wrote a book, simply titled *Iroquois*. It's no stretch to put two and two together here and accept the fact that Mary Moulthrop truly had contact with Seneca Indians and did, indeed, get the name "Onanda" from them.

Unlike today, when folks can rent a cabin at Onanda Park and enjoy their stay however they wish, Mary Moulthrop's Camp Onanda was a disciplined but educational experience in nature. It was designed for adult workingwomen.

Keenly aware of her father's success with disciplined school programs and his influence at the Natural Science Camp at Tichenor Point (see Ray Henry's book *The Natural Science Camp at Tichenor Point* for more about that camp), Mary set the direction for Camp Onanda's workingwomen in a like fashion.

A typical day would begin early, with all campers participating in Mary's calisthenics class. Mary made sure that meals were well balanced and oversaw the kitchen staff and waitresses. They served three nourishing meals a day, including a full breakfast, dinner at noon and a lighter meal in the evening.

Even the more relaxed evening activities around the campfire were carefully orchestrated to keep a consistent flow. From the moment the girls woke until the designated lights out at 10:30 p.m., Mary Moulthrop created structure.

Lights out was taken as seriously as any of the rules, and if rules were broken, Mary would have something to say to those not keeping them.

Mary was involved with every aspect of camp, from contracting with local farmers, kitchen staff and teachers for classes to providing campers with a wonderful experience. She most definitely was a chip off her father's block and gave Camp Onanda a solid beginning.

While Mary was the visible leader at Camp Onanda, there were many women in Rochester working equally hard. Mrs. Henry A. Strong, president of the YWCA at this time, not only provided some enthusiastic and needed drive in making the YWCA a strong association for women but also gave large sums of money. The Strong family was well known to all Rochesterians of the time. Mr. Henry Alvah Strong was a native Rochesterian, a Civil War veteran and the first president of the Eastman Kodak Company. The family made large donations to the teaching hospital at the University of Rochester Medical School. That hospital, Strong Hospital, retains the family name to this very day. Henry even accompanied his wife and other ladies of the YWCA to assess the Foster property and it's potential purchase. Mrs. Charles H. Babcock, Mrs. Frank P. Crouch, Miss Sara Hyatt, Mrs. Harper Sibley and so many others contributed to the YWCA's growth and Camp Onanda's success.

Another article from a Rochester newspaper in July 1913 reported the intent of the YWCA. It was determined to purchase a permanent place to be used as a summer retreat. Though not spelled correctly in this article, the YWCA already referred to this land as Camp Onanda.

Talk about forward-thinking businesswomen! Despite all the restrictions placed on women of the early 1900s, nothing seemed to stop them. The YWCA women rounded up the legal support needed and found the finances to take ownership of the land they wanted. Without their husbands, the land could not have been purchased, but we know the rest of that story!

It would be remiss not to share the Foster family's role in the history of Camp Onanda. The Foster family has a long and wonderful history in Canandaigua as a village, town and city, beginning around 1840 with the arrival of William Knibb Foster.

William Knibb Foster set up a boot factory and resided on the upper floors at 355 South Main Street, Canandaigua. The 1850 federal census names William K.; his wife, Mary Fay; their five children; and five workers as residents. The five Foster children—two boys and three girls—ranged in age from nine-year-old William L. to not-yet-one John T.. The Foster girls, Harriet E., Sarah F. and Mary would marry Civil War veterans, and William L. Foster would become the important link with Camp Onanda's history.

William L. Foster graduated from the Canandaigua Academy and then joined his granduncle, Charles Foster, in the book business. The Fosters traveled throughout the United States and Britain, purchasing and selling ready-made leather-bound libraries to wealthy families.

William Lewis married Anna Louisa "Eliza" Gasper in 1871 and settled into a home, which included Eliza's desired white picket fence, at 98 North Main Street in Canandaigua. With marriage came a career change. Though literature remained a passion for William throughout his life, in 1872, he purchased two large farms with lakefront property on the west side of the Canandaigua Lake. William went from bookseller to fruit farmer.

William and Eliza start their family, with daughter Mary Pauline arriving in 1875 and son William Lewis Foster Jr. arriving two years later.

Fostoria, about three miles from the town of Canandaigua, would become the Foster apple farm and thrive for over one hundred years. At Shale Rock, five miles south of Fostoria, William would build a large family home, surrounded by peach trees on the lakefront land. This would become Camp Onanda.

Pause for a moment and try to imagine 1872 around the shore and hills sloping toward the lake. Transportation was by horse (horse and wagon when possible) or by foot. Roads were surely narrow and, sometimes, mere dirt and rocky paths generally maintained by the folks who used them. To be eight miles from a town (Shale Rock) or even three miles (the fruit farm) from a railroad would be difficult at best for a farmer wanting to sell crops. Thus, the first steamboat on Canandaigua Lake, *The Lady of the Lake*, was launched in 1827 and was the beginning of a competitive, and needed, transportation business for those living around or visiting the lake. People, products and mail were delivered and picked up well into age of the automobile. Many of the skeletons of these wonderful steamboats rest in the depths of Canandaigua Lake. There are many detailed sources for you to learn more about Canandaigua Lake steamboats.

Meanwhile, by 1900, William Sr. had a large home built at Fostoria that was used as a packinghouse and residence for many of the workers. William Jr., now twenty-three, was in charge of shipping. Packaged fruit was picked up by boat at Fostoria, steamboat stop five. Fruit was then delivered to the pier at Canandaigua where trains awaited the packaged fruit to carry it to distant destinations.

At Shale Rock or at Fostoria, a flag would be raised to alert the steamboat pilot to stop. The color of the flag set out initially indicated which steamboat should stop. But, like all businesses, the steamboat businesses on Canandaigua Lake got highly competitive, and boats would race to flags regardless of color. Once a flag of any color was raised at any stop, it was considered fair game for any available steamboat.

William Jr., with a firm grasp of fruit farming learned at his father's side, set out to see the country and established himself in the citrus business. By the early 1900s, William Jr. owned two citrus groves outside St. Petersburg, Florida. At a yacht club in Florida, he met Amanda Cage Powell and married her in November 1905. The wedding gift from his father and mother was

Camp Onanda, 1919. *Courtesy of the Fisher/Knisley Collection.*

Camp Onanda arrival point, 1919. *Courtesy of the Fisher/Knisley Collection.*

Fostoria. This gift of the fruit farm on Canandaigua Lake made William Jr. and his wife two of the first "Florida Snowbirds," as they spent spring and summer as residents in Canandaigua and fall and winter as residents of Florida. With the passing of William Sr. in 1914, William Jr. sold off the citrus farms and took up permanent residence in Canandaigua, where William Jr. and Amanda would raise their two-year-old son Robert and take full responsibility for Fostoria.

On December 1, 1919, after the passing of William L. Foster Sr. in 1914 and his wife, Anna, on July 3, 1919, the land that had first been purchased by Harvey C. Foster in 1869 from William Cox and then conveyed to William L. Foster Sr. was now rightfully and legally "indentured" to the "Young Women's Christian Association of Rochester, N.Y., a domestic corporation of Number 190 Franklin Street, in the City of Rochester, New York." No longer having to rent the vacation houses just next door, the YWCA could now transform this land into Camp Onanda.

This purchase included twelve and a half acres, with peach trees, the Foster home, a tenant house, a storage/loading building on the shore and several smaller storage buildings. The Foster home would now be known as Hill House as a way of thanking Agnes Hill for her large financial donation to the YWCA specifically for purchasing the property. Hill House would be the center of all things Camp Onanda until the summer of 1922.

It was interesting to note in the legal document conveying this land to the YWCA of Rochester that the Foster children William and Mary added: "The party of the second part (that being the YWCA) shall quietly enjoy the said premises." It would seem that this "quiet" would be disrupted when it became primarily a camp for youngsters.

At any rate, the summer of 1919 must have been one of celebration for everyone involved with the purchase of this land. Even those uninvolved could see a change on the west side of Canandaigua Lake. Anyone taking a steamboat ride saw Camp Onanda taking its place.

3

Onanda's Decades

THE ROARING TWENTIES AT CAMP ONANDA

Warren G. Harding was president at the start of the decade, and Herbert Hoover resided in the White House at the decade's close. The population of the United States was over 100 million for the first time (106,521,537, of which 2,132,000 were unemployed). It took thirteen days to reach California from New York by car. Lindbergh flew solo across the Atlantic, as did Amelia Earhart. The first commercial radio broadcast aired, and Prohibition began. The lie detector was invented, and insulin and penicillin were discovered. The first Olympic winter games were held, and Babe Ruth made homerun history. The professional football league, golf tours and tennis circuits were organized. The first Mickey Mouse cartoon was presented, and *Winnie-the-Pooh* was published. The decade began with women gaining the right to vote on August 18, 1920 and ended with the stock market crash beginning on October 24, 1929.

While the young, single workingwoman of Rochester who came to Camp Onanda in the Roaring Twenties were likely grounded and determined, they had to be influenced or at least intrigued by the powerful changes unfolding for all American women. Yes, these women of the 1920s would be dubbed "new women." Since Susan B. Anthony had been a speaker and honored guest at the opening of the new YWCA building on North Clinton Avenue in Rochester in June 1898, it would seem that Rochester's women felt more connected to the women's rights movement than many.

As the summer of 1920 ended, women had finally won the right to vote. It had been a long fight, and there was a visible change in women. The general attitude of the time was that women should not work outside the home if their husbands held jobs. However, at the same time, public acceptance of wage-earning jobs for young, unmarried women was growing. No longer limited to jobs in mills or as domestics, women were going to work at clerical offices, retail shops and department stores and in more varied roles in industry.

With a better income came an image and attitude change among women. Fashion changed as women began to wear short skirts (showing their calves, oh my!), short hair and makeup. The close-fitting cloche hat and flesh-colored stockings with decorative shoes became the bee's knees, the ultimate for the new woman.

Though moderate in comparison to the attitude and changes in young women of the Roaring Twenties nationally, change was apparent at Camp Onanda as well. Gals wore middies and knickers more often than not. Many wore their hair cut short. Most had sneakers for hiking and sport activities. It's unlikely that many bothered with makeup, but they likely decked themselves out for stunt nights.

Camp Onanda of the summer of 1920 really only had the Foster home, now renamed Hill House, for camper accommodations. With clear ownership of the land, the YWCA was driven to improve this situation, and a new dormitory was its dream. A large donation made by Edith Babcock for this building made that dream come true, and because of this enormous donation, the building would be simply named Babcock Hall.

By the end of the summer of 1920, building began. The 136-foot-long two-story dormitory that sprang from the shale shore of Camp Onanda was designed by Rochester architect Edwin S. Gordon. Gordon had just started building the Eastman Theater but must have honored the request that likely came from Mrs. Henry Strong and Mrs. Charles Babcock for his design. Henry Strong of Eastman Kodak Company and Charles Babcock, president of a local bank and highly involved with railroads, were influential businessmen. Their wives' request to Mr. Gordon was heard.

Workers started in earnest at the close of summer activities in 1920, hoping to complete Babcock Hall for the summer of '21. Materials and workers were often brought down the lake by steamboat. Hammers hummed and workmen hustled to have this huge and wonderful new dormitory ready for the campers.

When the last nails were about to be struck and the finishing touches completed, disaster struck as the workmen took a weekend off. On Friday, June 11, 1921, knowing they were nearly finished, the workmen left their tools to return on Monday to finish this huge project.

On Monday, June 13, 1921, the *Geneva Daily Times* ran an article titled "Camp Building of Y.W.C.A. at Canandaigua Lake Burns to Ground, $5,000 Damage." On Saturday, the article explained, a party of "automobilists" apparently stopped by the camp, built a bonfire on the beach and neglected to extinguish it before departing.

When the workmen returned on June 13, they found their work and their tools in ashes. From a seemingly careless accident, Babcock Hall was brought to a smoldering pile of total destruction. Nothing could be salvaged. What would this horrific loss mean to the future of Camp Onanda?

It is unlikely that Onanda was used much during the summer of 1921. Hill House had not been damaged, so small groups might have come for a weekend getaway, but this is not clear. What is clear is that Babcock Hall rose out of those ashes like a phoenix to welcome the young workingwomen of Rochester to Onanda the very next summer. Once again, Edith Babcock stepped up to help and donated the needed finances to rebuild. Camp Onanda would not be denied its place on the west shore of Canandaigua Lake.

AERIAL VIEW, ROCHESTER YWCA CAMP ONANDA, CANANDAIGUA, N. Y.

The new Babcock Hall, 1922. *Author's collection.*

Permission was given to Mr. Brennan to purchase three Yale locks for the doors at Onanda and to make arrangements for the necessary plowing and uprooting of trees, the cost not to exceed $25.00. The five young maple trees were accepted with real thanks as the gift of Mrs. Speddy and Mr. Brennan was asked to get in touch with the tree expert at Canandaigua who would give advice not only as to the setting out of these trees but also concerning the condition of all the peach trees and the two large pine trees before the farmhouse.

There were issues to resolve at Onanada. *Courtesy of the University of Rochester.*

Camp Onanda of 1922 now had great accommodations, and it also had fine food. Three meals a day were prepared by a cook with dietary knowledge and were served by waitresses. Breakfast would always include some sort of fruit, juice, cocoa and a choice of cereal or eggs, with muffins and jelly costing $0.40. For $0.60, dinner was the big meal and could be anything from fish to beef with vegetables and dessert. Supper was lighter, but always balanced, and cost $0.40. If staying for a weekend, which was considered to be Saturday after lunch to Monday after breakfast, the entire cost, including accommodations, was $2.00. A full week would cost $10.50.

With ownership came new demands. A committee to deal with camp needs and expenses was formed. This smaller group included Mary Moulthrop and others who regularly spent time at Onanda in the summer. The committee's primary goal was to keep Camp Onanda safe and solvent, which almost always meant that there was a need or issue to be resolved.

Produce, as often as was possible, came from local farmers. There were fruit trees all around the camp land (primarily peaches) that were used by the camp and surplus sold for additional camp income. Mr. Brennan, father of the camp's caretaker, provided milk. Most often, local folks were hired for cleaning and laundry needs. So right from the start, Camp Onanda was connected with the local folks in a positive way.

While Babcock Hall was a wonderful shelter and Hill House offered up incredible meals, there still was no hot water available to those staying at Camp Onanda. The lake remained the primary means of cleaning clothes and maintaining personal hygiene. It was, after all, a camp.

Electricity was provided by batteries in Hill House and other buildings on the property. Some bare bulb pendant lighting was installed in Babcock Hall using those batteries as well. In the 1925 executive committee notes, we learn that at the end of the summer, batteries would no longer be necessary. Electricity would be extended from the town of Canandaigua to Onanda. Surely this would mean hot water for all and more lights.

Usually around mid-June, Camp Onanda was prepared to greet weekend and short-term visitors. Around the first of July, blocks of time were set aside for the entire camp experience for YWCA boarders in Rochester. For at least three weeks of the summer, young women would sign up for at least a week's stay, where they would be involved with classes in nature, drawing, handcrafts, swimming, archery, tennis and boating.

Developing a safe and structured camp experience takes planning and effort, and the YWCA had the leadership to provide for those needs. Mary Moulthrop remained a driving force, along with Agnes Rix Kidder, who would push for and develop a program for young girls' regular use of Onanda.

Near the close of the Roaring Twenties, the costs of camp were firmly established for Camp Onanda. A weekend at Camp Onanda cost slightly less than one at Camp Wacona, perhaps because it took more effort and cost to get to Onanda.

COSTS:

Weekend	$2.00	Breakfast	$0.40
Full week	$10.50	Dinner (regular)	$0.60
Single day	$1.50	Dinner (holiday or Sunday)	$0.75
One night	$0.55	Supper (regular)	$0.40
Holiday	[no price listed]	Special supper	$0.75 and up
Weekend	$3.50		

Counselors in the '20s actually looked about the same as the staffs of future summers. However, originally, they were selected through various YWCAs around the country. These gals had special areas of expertise and often came from out of state. Agnes Rix Kidder was one such recruited gal. Born on April 6, 1890, in Berlin, St. Claire County, Michigan, Agnes was fully involved with Onanda in the summer of '22.

The Rochester YWCA "found" Agnes at the National Training School of the YWCA in Manhattan, New York, around 1920. She was quickly hired as director of the girls' work department in Rochester and would eventually become the executive director of the Rochester YWCA.

Agnes was a perfect match for the YWCA's goals and programs. She was a single workingwoman and so was well aware of the struggles and interests

The 1922 counselors. *Courtesy of the Albert R. Stone Collection, RMSC.*

of Rochester's workingwomen housed by the YWCA. She, too, benefitted from being the daughter of a strong woman. Agnes's mother was a widow, like Marian Crouch's mother, and managed to provide for her children well. Yes, Agnes was completely aware of the needs of single women.

It is apparent that Agnes Rix Kidder flung her energy into Camp Onanda's beginnings and opened it up to girls of all ages. By 1926, she had developed a summer program for school-aged girls at Onanda. Three weeks were designated for youngsters only. Agnes developed the classes, hired the staff, grouped the girls into units and oversaw the entire Onanda experience for the young girls.

These first counselors were simply instructors. They led classes in archery, tennis, swimming, boating, photography, handcrafts, nature studies, writing and the like. They did not have a group of campers for whom they were responsible, as future counselors would. They, like all generations of counselors to come, helped out in organizing all sorts of activities and likely with maintenance of materials and grounds to some degree.

Campers—almost all visitors, actually—still arrived at Camp Onanda by steamboat in this decade. For those from Rochester or other distant cities

Archery class, 1922. *Courtesy of the Albert R. Stone Collection, RMSC.*

Can you even begin to fathom how heavy these woolen swimsuits would be once wet? It's a wonder that gals learned to swim. *Courtesy of the Albert R. Stone Collection, RMSC.*

and towns, this still meant a train or trolley ride to the Canandaigua pier with all their gear. What changed in this decade was that this trip was being made by school-aged girls, too!

What does one bring to camp in the 1920s? Since there was no laundry facility, either enough clothing for the entire stay was brought or few clothes were packed and washed in the lake at some point. Bedding was still provided and was likely never changed during the stay unless the camper washed it. The local women employed to do the camp laundry did this once a week or when the camper left.

If you have spent time camping, you know that many summer mornings in New York remain a tad nippy. Unless an early morning fire had been set in Babcock Hall's fireplace, the day started with a blast of cold. Campers would need warm clothes, and in the '20s that meant heavy stockings, sturdy shoes and sneakers and sweaters, as well as clothing for warmer days and, of course a swimsuit.

The lake was a major draw for anyone living in a city. Camp Onanda took full advantage of its waterfront and kept the younger campers safe around it by making swimming class mandatory for all. Learning to swim is a wonderful goal, but in the 1920s, in a woolen bathing suit, this had to be a major feat.

OFF TO CAMP!

Try to imagine that it's 1926. You're twelve years old and live in Rochester. Your parents have read many articles in the local paper about Camp Onanda or maybe your Sunday school teacher or a girlfriend has told you about the camp. You ask your parents if you could go to Onanda, and they agree to register you for a session. How exciting is that?

You've never been away from home for any extended time without your parents. Your parents don't have a car, and the camp is forty miles away. What do you bring? How will you get there?

Once you register for camp, things begin to fall into place. You go to the YWCA with your mom and get a physical examination. You're weighed and measured, and your mom answers questions about your general health. This is done to make sure that you are healthy enough to enjoy all the activities at camp. You're asked about your interests, if you know how to swim and what you hope to do at camp.

You passed this entrance requirement and now have a list of things you should and shouldn't bring to camp, as well as the instructions for getting to camp.

Two weeks later, on Saturday afternoon, your bags are packed, and you're waiting with a group of sixty-nine other girls and their parents at the trolley station in downtown Rochester. The YWCA has engaged two private cars for this leg of the trip. This was called the "excursion option." Both cars are reserved just for the campers and will go all the way to the city pier at Canandaigua Lake with girls and gear rather than stop at Niagara Street in Canandaigua.

You are among the very first of the young girls to be invited to experience "a week of outdoor life at Camp Onanda." There will be three such sessions this summer, but you are in the first. Even though you're excited about this, you're also just a tad nervous. For some reason, you're now not sure you want to leave your parents. You can't even explain your feelings and almost tell your parents you don't want to go. Instead of voicing your fears, you ask your mom for the millionth time if you have all your stuff. Your parents laugh and assure you that you have everything but the kitchen sink in your small trunk.

Miss Kidder, the camp director, is mingling among the girls and parents, and ten counselors are cheerfully doing the same. Now you're getting more and more excited again. You just learned that you'll be taking this special trolley all the way to a pier at Canandaigua and then will be getting on a large boat called the *Eastern Star* for an eight-mile ride down the lake to the camp. You've never been on a big boat. Heck, you've never been on boat of any kind.

Miss Butterfield, one of the counselors, notices that you're a bit nervous and puts you more at ease by telling you that she will be teaching photography. She's going to show you how to compose a picture and even how to develop and print the pictures. She introduces you to another counselor, Miss Elsie Buritt, who will be teaching archery.

Miss Buritt has been to Onanda many summers and tells you about the glen and all the great activities that await you. When you ask about the sleeping situation, she explains that everyone will be in the same huge dorm and quickly adds that it's a very safe and comfortable place.

At 1:15 p.m., you give your parents one last hug and kiss and hop on the trolley with the hint of a tear but still excited somehow. Miss Kidder organizes the seating, and you're off. As waves and final shouts of farewell are given, Miss Kidder begins to share the rules of travel and camp. She's really nice but also very firm about the rules. The counselors are all introduced, and

The trolley to Canandaigua. *Author's collection.*

each shares what she will be teaching. For a few minutes, everyone watches the scenery rush by as Miss Kidder tells where you are and what to look for. It amazes you how quickly the buildings and houses of the city seem to disappear and endless woods take over in every direction.

About an hour into the ride, Miss Bernice Milner, another counselor, tells a story called "The Legend of Bare Hill." It was about the Seneca Indians who once lived on Canandaigua Lake. At first, you thought it was a story about bears, but you laugh when you realize it has nothing to do with bears. You're also relieved to know that there are no bears around Canandaigua or Camp Onanda.

Finally, just as the trolley seats are beginning to feel uncomfortable, more houses come into view. You've reached the town of Canandaigua and soon are traveling down the city's main street. Up ahead you can see the lake.

The pier is a bustling place. There are steamboats docked and men unloading crated fruit from them to the waiting trains. It seems just as loud as the public market back home but not as big.

And there it is. The *Eastern Star* is on the opposite side of the pier from the larger boats that are being unloaded. It's hard to describe, but it's longer than the trolley car but maybe not as wide. You honestly can't imagine how it can hold everyone and all the luggage. Miss Kidder laughs at your doubt and assures you that everything will fit, including campers. You are sort of excited to get on board and sort of nervous about it too. I mean, you can swim, but this lake is huge.

The *Eastern Star* steamer took girls to camp. *Courtesy of the Town of Canandaigua Collection.*

The captain of the *Eastern Star* helps each camper aboard, asking each girl's name and just making everyone feel special and safe. He has a great smile and reminds you of your dad. Then, you realized you aren't with your parents and get a little nervous. You almost begin to cry. Almost magically, Miss Kidder is at your side, pointing out new wonders and assuring you that your parents will be so excited to hear all about what you are seeing when you get home. You don't know how she does it, but Miss Kidder gets you all excited about camp again and gives you the idea to write a journal about your Onanda adventure.

Yes, simply getting to camp was huge part of the adventure, no matter what year a camper arrived at Onanda.

At the close of Onanda's first decade, Camp Onanda was sometimes a vacation location for older single women and other times a summer camp for young girls. Both groups enjoyed activities geared toward them, and while they weren't there at the same time, both groups found and made wonderful memories.

THE GREAT DEPRESSION AND DUST BOWL DECADE

1930s

This decade begins with Herbert Hoover at the helm of the United States government, though he then quickly turned the tiller over to Franklin D. Roosevelt to guide the country. Construction of the Empire State Building was completed, and it was opened for business, as were the Golden Gate Bridge and the Hoover Dam. Zippo lighters were introduced, air conditioning invented and the cheeseburger created. Dick Tracy debuted in comic strips, Parker Brothers began sales of *Monopoly*, and Orson Wells scared radio audiences with his broadcast of *The War of the Worlds*. Since the fall of the stock market in 1929, the income of average American families had dropped by 40 percent. Horrible drought turned middle states into a dust bowl, devastating the nation's farmers. The Social Security Act was started to ensure an income for the elderly, and the Civilian Conservation Corps was established to give young men jobs. Likely hoping to inspire the people of the United States, the decade began with the "The Star Spangled Banner" officially becoming the national anthem (March 3, 1931) and ended with the United States declaring its neutrality in the European war after Germany invaded Poland (September 1939).

The Great Depression was a horrific economic crush worldwide. While the Depression had long-reaching causes, the fall of the U.S. stock market affected rich and poor. International trade dropped by more than 50 percent, and unemployment rose 25 percent. Industry was especially hard hit, construction virtually halted and farming prices fell by nearly 60 percent. Then, too, Mother Nature hit the farmers of the Midwest with a draught so bad that fields became barren, the top soil blown to places unknown. It was definitely a depressing time for millions.

In 1930, Rochester's population was 328,132, making it the twenty-third-largest city in the United States. By this time, it was also an industrial city, and that meant struggling. Eastman Kodak Company, Bausch & Lomb, Gleason Works and many smaller companies providing thousands of jobs were hard pressed to keep all employees working. Still, each company held its ground, but workers suffered. George Eastman knew well of financial struggles, and rather than lay off workers, he cut back hours and implemented shift working. Someone who may have worked five days a week might be cut to three days one week and two the next. This meant lower wages but also made more jobs for men who had lost their jobs at other places. This change also meant that production would continue at Eastman Kodak Company. The industries and people of Rochester would survive, but daily life was full of change and uncertainty.

And when times get tough, charitable organizations hear the calls of despair and work all the harder to ease some of the pain. The YWCA of Rochester was no exception. It adjusted the rent for its residents, conducted the Leisure Time School to give training and recreation to unemployed girls, established cafeterias where rounded meals could be purchased at lower costs and simply was there to help and give those who were struggling some sense of support and normalcy. That means, of course, that Camp Onanda would welcome vacationing single women and young girls as usual.

As the 1930s began, Babcock Hall was only eight years old and well maintained. It easily housed eighty girls who were usually broken into eight groups of ten with a "ranger" in charge of each group. Hill House, too, was in fine shape to provide meals, so camp flowed in its usual manner. Girls hiked the glen, put on skits, wrote poetry and enjoyed all the activities a lakefront camp could offer. Onanda was busy despite the economic upheaval around it.

Normalcy and healthy fun was Camp Onanda. All girls were welcome to participate, and parents were glad for the distraction camp offered their girls.

In her article for the *Democrat & Chronicle*, Julia M. Traver shared her findings at Onanda. She wrote:

> *There is the freedom of personal initiative in the camp, although there is a well arranged program. The point is that each girl who spends her allotted time there lives a life free from regimentation and along the line of her own special interest, but she is not permitted to become unsocial or antisocial. In fact, a few hours after a girl has arrived at camp she loses any antisocial attitudes she may have had. One of the striking things about the modern girl is her quick adaptability to situations and her easy poise, two traits that appear to be particularly characteristic at this camp.*

Traver goes on to describe the varied attire of the girls, the activities on the waterfront and the building of what she called an aquarium. She explains how the girls did all the work of digging out a four-foot-deep, five-foot-square hole that they blocked up and then pouring the cement that lined it entirely on their own. She reported that, "The job has been [so] neatly and successfully done that any man could be proud of it."

Character, Health Building Provided at Y.W.C.A. Camp

Recreational Facilities One of Features Of Onanda, On West Side of Canandaigua Lake—Girls Build Aquarium, Bird Bath

By JULIA M. TRAVER

Snuggled in th hills out where the air blows crisp and clean across Canandaigua Lake, nestles Camp Onanda. This camp, located about eight miles south of Can- ture was being taken up stepped Master Gerald (Bingy) Brennan who, in the picture assumed the role of leader. "Bingy" is a son of the caretaker of the camp and its

An article about the YWCA camp. *Courtesy of the University of Rochester.*

Character building, indeed. And with such articles regularly appearing in the Rochester newspapers, it's not surprising that Camp Onanda was always attended to capacity. In the 1930s, that meant that for four weeks each summer, the camp was filled with the laughter and activities of 240 girls. Unfortunately, almost as many girls were put on a waiting list and never got to camp. Something needed to change so more girls could experience Onanda.

Records don't show the exact costs, but the chapters of the YWCA somehow managed to raise the money for two large building additions to Camp Onanda in the '30s. The first was a fairly large cabin some distance from Babcock, to the south and nearer the road, that could house an additional twenty campers. The second was a greatly needed meeting and rainy day recreation hall. These new additions were announced in the 1938 Onanda brochure.

On a bright cheerful Thursday in June 1938, before Onanda's gate was open to the girls for summer camp, a truly wonderful ceremony was held to dedicate the new recreation hall.

Two hundred women, representing the twenty-seven chapters of the Rochester YWCA, gathered to dedicate the Crouch Memorial Hall at Onanda. The late Marian Elizabeth McLeod Crouch had been the president

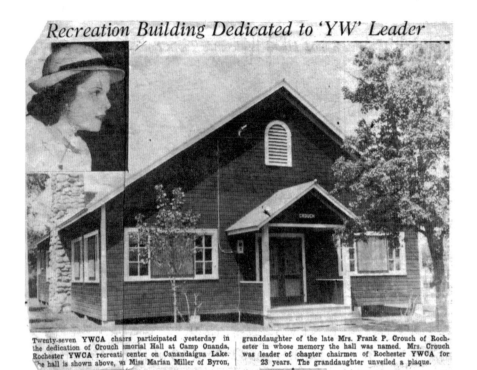

Recreation Building Dedicated to 'YW' Leader

Twenty-seven YWCA chairs participated yesterday in the dedication of Crouch Memorial Hall at Camp Onanda, Rochester YWCA recreation center on Canandaigua Lake. The hall is shown above, with Miss Marian Miller of Byron, granddaughter of the late Mrs. Frank P. Crouch of Rochester in whose memory the hall was named. Mrs. Crouch was leader of chapter chairmen of Rochester YWCA for 23 years. The granddaughter unveiled a plaque.

YW Dedicates Camp Onanda Memorial Hall

Canandaigua—In a perfect setting of green lawns besides the blue waters of Canandaigua Lake 27 YWCA chapters participated in the main building to conclude the girls followed by a week's camping period for colored girls of the program. Among the guests of honor were Mrs. Helen Crouch Miller, Byron, Clarissa Street branch under the direction of Miss Estelle Fitzger

The Crouch Hall dedication. *Courtesy of Helen Smith.*

of the YWCA chapters for twenty-three years. She was instrumental in the growth and direction of the association since its beginning and always championed Camp Onanda. It was truly fitting that this wonderful recreation hall be named in her memory.

Crouch Hall had a huge fireplace built with lake rocks. A stage where camper and staff shows and drama of all kinds would unfold was a great bonus. The hall was spacious and could accommodate the entire camp population for special events or rainy day activities. Crouch Hall would also set the standard for the style of future building projects and has been the most well-used building at Onanda since it was built.

Crouch's granddaughter and namesake, Marian Miller, unveiled a plaque in her grandmother's honor on that lovely day in 1938. She had attended Onanda as a youngster, as would her daughter. Marian's

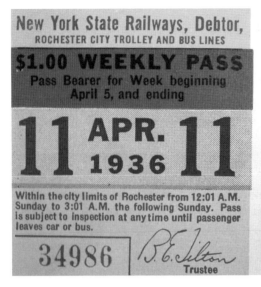

A trolley ticket promoting Onanda. *Author's collection.*

daughter, Helen Smith, today remembers well her summers at Camp Onanda and remains awed and rightfully proud of all her great-grandmother did for women through her work with the YWCA. The Crouch women would be touched by Onanda from 1906 to 1962. As significant improvements were made around Camp Onanda throughout the years, Crouch Hall was the addition that truly united campers and counselors each summer and provided those lifelong memories. If only this building could talk.

Just as today you see advertisements on local buses, the YWCA used the Rochester city trolley to keep the word out about Camp Onanda. Several weeks prior to the opening of camp, the weekly trolley passes donned a pitch for the rider to send their girl to camp.

Parents of potential campers were daily aware of Camp Onanda if they took the trolley to work. Then, too, their girls must have seen this trolley pass and pestered for a chance to go to camp. But newspaper articles and trolley passes were not the only means the YWCA used to get the word out.

Fairly detailed blips about Onanda were sent to the local radio station, WHAM, and broadcast each year. To hear about camp from a local radio personality must have kept girls listening. In 1936, this is how the radio announcement began.

Everyone keeps telling us that really spring is just around the corner, and we are all anxious enough to turn that corner. After spring comes summer and that means "happy days are here again"—also that "camping days are here again."

Now is the time we want to think about our plans for summer and for those camping days. With many of you, summer means Camp Onanda, the YWCA camp located on the west shore of Canandaigua Lake, about eight miles from Canandaigua.

This radio blip was a full page and a half, no thirty second ad for sure.

By at least 1938, the YWCA had started using brochures to entice parents to send their girls to camp. These brochures were quite detailed and were likely found at local churches and some locations around town like the trolley stations. Of course, any girl or parent could get one upon request at the YWCA.

More often than not, word of mouth was as powerful as any of the publicity in terms of bringing girls to camp. Neighbors shared, classmates shared, gals in Sunday schools shared, so it's hardly a stretch to see how friends would end up at camp together.

Anticipation built as the names of those attending Onanda were published in the newspaper.

For three summers, 1937 through 1939, Estyne Levi of Milburn Street, Rochester, was among the names listed in the newspaper.

Estyne was the only child of Berthold and Pearl Levi and eleven years old the

---

Tel. Main 900

Onanda Gets First Lot Of Campers

Sunny skies greeted the initial encampment at Onanda, YWCA camp on Canandaigua Lake which opened its season Saturday with a record enrollment.

Included are the following local girls: Altrud Betz, Margaret Betz, Ruth Lee Cohn, Ruth Soble, Marjorie Lanni, Patricia Hanna, Ann Williams, Barbara Butler, Estyne Levi, Theilma Neiman, Ruth Betz, Suzanne Levin, Martha Stonebraker, Dorothy Blake, Catherine Brennan, Marjorie Weisberg, Janet Griswold, Phyllis Wronker, Sylvia Barber, Gloria Knickerbocker.

Carolyn Barber, John Martin, Alice Holman, Jeanne Marie Davis, Joy Churchin, Joan Harding, Janet Quinn, Anne Collins, Janet Horton, Joan Humbert.

Sue Cooper, Ann Hartman, June Scheer, Jean Vande Vate, Anna Barber, Doris Bailey, Ruth Carroll, Marjorie Cohen, Nancy Farnum, Ellen Garson.

Carolyn Houck, Jean Klein, Barbara Leffert, Joyce Levy, Nancy

Campers sign up. *Courtesy of the University of Rochester.*

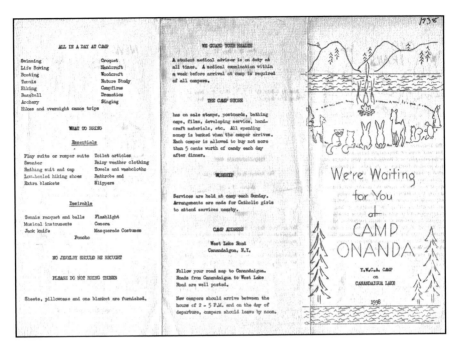

Onanda in 1938. *Courtesy of the Fisher/Knisley Collection.*

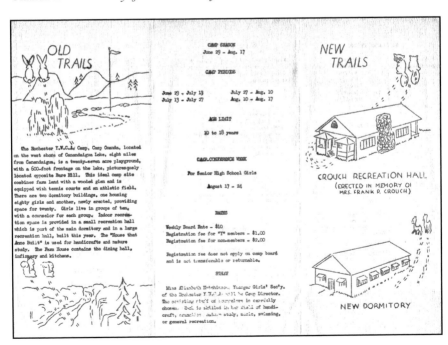

It cost only ten dollars a week to attend camp. *Courtesy of the Fisher/Knisley Collection.*

first time she ventured off to Camp Onanda. Estyne, called "Teeney" by friends and family, did not set off alone on this adventure but with her friend Ruth "Ruthie" Lee Cohn of Brighton.

Both the Levis and Cohns were looking for a safe and fun experience for their daughters. Knowing, already, of the changes taking place in Europe, they wanted to shelter their girls from worry as long as they could. The Cohns still had family in Russia, the Levis in Austria, and through letter exchanges the name Hitler was already too familiar to them. A week away at such a well-known camp sounded ideal for their girls.

The eleven year olds had a blast! Ruthie loved art and enjoyed the many ways to express that love at camp. There were art classes, craft classes and creating backdrops for skits to fill her days. Teeney got involved with the dance, music and drama groups. She also dabbled in photography and made a special album that she kept among her treasured collections for the rest of her life. Both girls learned to swim, cook over an open fire and catch fish. They made new friends that would be kept, like Teeney's album, throughout their lives.

Despite the additional cabins built in the early 1930s, Camp Onanda was still forced to turn girls away. The camp committee wanted to change this and began a serious study and discussion of how to provide more options for youngsters' use of Onanda.

The working, single women for whom the camp was initially designed were still using the camp, but they simply didn't have as much time off from work to vacation at Onanda. The demands on the workingwomen were a catalyst for the YWCA to cut back its scheduled programs at Onanda for them and increase the options for young girls' camping. Ever aware of the differences in interests of high school seniors in its city programs from their younger counterparts, the YWCA came up with a plan for Onanda's use. Now, the teens would have an exclusive, one-week session at camp. Younger girls would be offered three different sessions, and still the workingwomen and rentals by churches, families and other groups could be accommodated.

Single workingwomen, high school girls and younger girls, family camping, senior camping (for older adults) and group rentals...how does an organization meet those needs? This was a challenge that YWCA leadership struggled with from the moment it opened the front gate to Camp Onanda.

In 1938 and 1939, the younger girls were offered three two-week sessions from the close of public schools in June through August. The last session of camp was set aside for high school seniors. This last summer session was only one week but allowed the YWCA senior high school club members to have exclusive use of Onanda. The weeks prior to and after the girls used camp were set up for the working gals and other interested groups. So it was that girls from ten to fifteen ruled the camp for six weeks right from the close of school and sixteen to eighteen year olds were in command for the last week of summer vacation. This plan would become an issue needing addressing as the older girls grumbled about their only option for camp.

Meanwhile, with all the struggles unfolding around the world during the '30s, Camp Onanda, this microscopic dot on the world, remained full of songs, laughter and hope.

THE HORRENDOUS '40s

A seemingly endless flow of horror dominated this decade. The Battle of Britain started it off. Two years later, Japan's attack on Pearl Harbor brought the United States into World War II. Franklin D. Roosevelt died before the war ended, and Harry S. Truman took the reins. The Manhattan Project began, and President Truman used its results on Hiroshima and Nagasaki, Japan. The power of the atomic bomb was horrifying. From the European front, we learned that the horror of the Holocaust was true. Six million Jewish men, women and children were dead. Even as such heaviness persists, some positives did unfold. Mount Rushmore was completed, and bikinis were introduced. Jeeps, Polaroid cameras, microwave ovens and the first computer were built, but only the ballpoint pen went on sale to the public. Dr. Spock's *The Common Book of Baby and Child Care* was published, Slinky Toys were on store shelves and T-shirts were introduced. At the close of the decade, both the United States and the Soviet Union had atomic bombs, and the cold war between the nations began.

As unspeakable things unfolded around the world, in industrial cities like Rochester, even more women joined the work force. John Hosking was a freshman at the University of Rochester heading for a future in medicine when Pearl Harbor was bombed. He closed his books and enlisted in the navy. He was a special medic on the USS *Harris* in the South Pacific. He and so many other men changed their plans or were drafted into service, leaving many positions at home empty. Women easily found jobs. They either filled the spaces left by men who enlisted or were placed at new jobs making things for the war effort. Tom Brokow would later refer to this generation of the 1940s and before as the Greatest Generation. Trust me, they were.

MEANWHILE, BACK AT CAMP ONANDA

In the midst of all this, the YWCA was busier than ever. Keeping to its mission, the YWCA was there for the women now working at all kinds of jobs. Rosie the Riveter was a national symbol of encouragement for those women working to support the war efforts, and Rochester had many "Rosies."

The stresses and strains on all families during the war were many, and all were affected. With more moms working and many dads also working or away at war, more children needed babysitters or safe places to wait for parents. The YWCA set up those safe places and held classes in babysitting. Whatever gaps and needs arose, efforts were made fill the gap or meet the need.

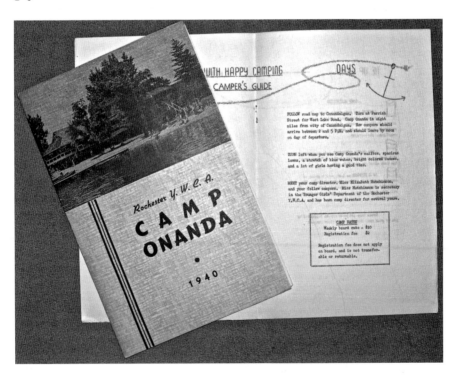

Onanda in the 1940s. *Courtesy of the Fisher/Knisley Collection.*

Clearly, with all that was going on in the world, Camp Onanda provided a brief escape from reality for young girls. Onanda would give campers a safe place to play and laugh but would also address the challenges left at home head on.

The camp brochure of 1940 started right off with a hook dangled for young girls:

> *SEASON 1940 at CAMP ONANDA lies ahead—fifty-six bright summer days from which to choose a camping period. More inviting than ever is this forty acre summer playground for girls, with its extensive waterfront overlooking rolling hills and clean sparking water, its ample dormitories and other trim buildings, several of which were built in the past two years.*
>
> *There are twelve buildings in all at Camp Onanda. These include, besides dormitories, buildings for handcrafts and nature study, an infirmary isolated from the campers' quarters, counselors's house, large open dining rooms, and well equipped kitchens. Prized most is Crouch Hall, recreation building with fireplace and stage.*
>
> *New this year is an "Adirondack Shelter," built on the hill high above the lake on camp property. Overnight hikers will use this when sudden showers come during the nights that they have planned to sleep out of doors.*

One cannot help but wonder how a brochure could boast of "fifty-six bright summer days" months before the opening of camp, but it was still a good hook. The cost of a session at Onanda in 1940 was ten dollars for weekly board and a two-dollar registration fee. A two-week session then would cost parents twenty-two dollars. Board included three meals a day, and a bed with sheets, a pillow and a blanket were still provided.

There were no additional charges except for purchases at the camp. If money was brought from home, it would be "banked" upon arrival. Campers would draw from their account for purchases of postcards, stationery, stamps, candy and other incidentals at the store. It was clearly stated that only five cents a day could be spent on candy. In 1940, that was a goodly amount! Eventually, the camp store would include popsicles, ice cream treats, sweatshirts, T-shirts and other camp memorabilia.

All camp brochures suggested what to bring to camp and what was not allowed. In 1940, in terms of clothing, this brochure listed, "playsuits, sweater, bathing suit, towels and washcloths, toilet articles, rainy weather clothing, bathrobe and slippers, low-heeled hiking shoes" and an extra blanket. Also included, as optional items, were "tennis racquet and balls, musical instruments, jack knife, poncho, flashlight, camera, and masquerade costumes." One should not come with jewelry or trunks.

I'm sure that you caught that sweatshirts and jackets are missing from the list of clothes, and I'm equally sure that you realize they weren't part of young girls' attire back then. Then, too, "playsuits" was not a term that girls in later years would even recognize!

A brochure about a camp also needed a hook for parents, and this one sure had that. What parent could ignore the words from "a recent volume" of the study of character education?

The back of the brochure read:

> *A Word to Parents*
>
> *From a recent volume on character education we quote:*
> *"Development of sturdy character and integrated personality is made a difficult and often an impossible task under the conditions of congested urban life…*
>
> *"The need for color, space and serenity is not satisfied by conditions of modern living."*
>
> *At CAMP ONANDA, the child finds color, space, serenity. Working and playing with a group make for a sense of security. At the same time the child gets individual attention and finds self-expression in things she likes to do.*
>
> *The program is colorful with room for satisfying attainments in dramatic productions, in crafts, in folk dancing, nature study and other activity.*

With the concerns of parents addressed, Camp Onanda jumped into the summer program of the 1940s.

Campers had a variety of activities to choose from, but one activity remained a must: swimming class. With that a given, they could then choose classes in tennis, hiking, baseball, archery, badminton, handcrafts, woodcrafts, nature study, dramatics, singing, photography, lifesaving and boating. Four or five classes were all a camper could include in her session at camp. Time simply didn't allow for more.

Each camp session, a camp newspaper was compiled. Articles, all written by campers for campers, related the happenings, achievements and gossip around camp. In 1940, a press room was added to the camp. Girls who signed on as reporters now had a designated work area.

Another option was to be a Pioneer. The Pioneers did big projects, like the aquarium described in the 1930s. The Pioneer project for 1940 was clearly described: "Last year a group of campers started an outdoor chapel project. Undoubtedly campers will continue it this year. It will take land clearing, landscaping, woodcraft, imagination."

Needless to suggest, there were always plenty of things to do at Onanda to fill a one- or two-week stay.

The eighty girls of Babcock were broken down into groups of ten, as were the gals in Wacona (that newer building that could accommodate twenty campers). In these smaller groups, with a counselor, they would set off on hikes and any number of other activities. No group did exactly the same

The war comes to camp. *Courtesy of the Fisher/ Knisley Collection.*

things, and that made for varied experiences. Class times were the same daily, as were two free swims, so smaller group activities were tucked in when time allowed.

In any decade at Camp Onanda, it was easy to be entirely absorbed by the fun and adventures in nature. Laughter, singing and learning were constant. Even so, the troubles of the world were addressed but in a positive way.

The camp brochure of 1943 firmly and clearly stated what camp would be about and reflected the tension and patriotism that was driving Americans.

Getting around Onanda in 1943. *Courtesy of the Fisher/Knisley Collection.*

Camp, in no sense, will be a mere summer resort this summer. All campers will be expected actively to participate in camp activities. Those who have the privilege of camping will certainly want to take advantage of the many opportunities to increase self-reliance and endurance and to be of service in the war effort.

A serious tone was set. While girls would sing and laugh and do silly things, every aspect of camp addressed patriotism.

Physical fitness—The ultimate success of any nation depends upon the physical strength of its people. Camp activities will follow the suggestions of the Physical Fitness program of the New York State War Council. The program will emphasize body building and conditioning and war emergency skills.

Creative activities—To free campers from the tensions and strains—music, dramatics, woodcraft and nature study. Service projects for USO and relocation centers are planned for the Craft House.

Cooperative living—The cooperation of each camper will be enlisted to give some time to help with preparation of vegetables for meals, cleaning and care of camp building and grounds, clearing of trails, etc.

There is a possibility of a camp garden or some work in gardens of nearby farmers. Campers at periods when berries are ripe may have an opportunity to help with this harvest.

Reading these descriptions in the twenty-first century might cause an eyebrow to rise or even a wee gasp to escape. It sounds almost harsh and not like the summer experience kids would flock to or parents would want their children involved with. But in 1943, every American family was touched by the war. They wanted their children strong, and children of World War II were eager to do their part and be strong for their parents. Enrollment was quickly filled.

The items that a camper would need at camp changed, too. No longer were "playsuits" mentioned first. Now it was shorts and slacks. The list was more specific, asking that soap, flashlights and a drinking cup or glass definitely be packed. Then the war came into the list of needs. Each camper was to bring a half pound of sugar for each week she attended, and it specifically stated that a sugar coupon was not acceptable. Campers had to bring the sugar. They also needed Ration Book 2 that would cover eleven points per week.

Yes, every girl old enough to go to Camp Onanda in 1943 knew exactly what this was all about. Rationing was a constant in their daily lives; they couldn't possibly miss it. The girls of Onanda knew their moms couldn't go into a store and buy as much sugar, butter or meat as she wanted, nor could their dads fill up the car with gasoline whenever he liked. Even if a family had the money to buy more, these things were rationed, which meant families were only allowed to buy small amounts of these things and only on

Rationing comes to Onanda. *Author's collection.*

certain days in some cases. After the Japanese attack on Pearl Harbor, the government started issuing ration books. Ration Book 1 was fondly called the "Sugar Book." A ration book had pages of patriot stamps that were presented when a rationed item was purchased. War ration books and tokens were issued to each American family, dictating how much gasoline, rubber products, sugar, meat, silk, shoes, nylon, coffee, butter and other items vital to the war effort could be purchased by civilians. Throughout World War II, Americans used four rationing books. A fifth book had been printed but was not distributed, as rationing had been lifted.

The YWCA was not exempt from rationing. In order to provide meals at camp, they needed sugar. Since rationing allowed for a half pound of sugar a week for each American, they asked that these rations come to camp. The request that campers needed Ration Book 2 was likely to assist in purchasing meat and other needs of the kitchen.

It seems likely that some girls couldn't come to camp because their families really needed the sugar and rationing stamps, but Camp Onanda was filled to capacity throughout the summer of '43. Patriotism and supporting the war effort were priorities. The brochure of 1943 definitely addressed the turmoil of war by promising to keep the girls of summer safe and strong. Even the songs sung reflected this difficult time.

The exact date of the end of World War II is not entirely agreed upon by historians, but with the German unconditional surrender on May 8, 1945, and Japan surrendering on August 15, 1945, most Americans felt Japan's surrender marked the end.

Camp in June 1945 must have had a lighter atmosphere, and in August, the laughter must have been louder and more easily shared.

The description of camp in 1947 truly tells it all:

> At Camp Onanda, campers and counselors work and play together in an atmosphere of fun and relaxation. In this small community of one hundred campers the camper experiences democracy in action. Living in the out of doors each camper has an opportunity to participate in plans and adventures of her own small dorm group, and in the plans for the total camp...
>
> The adventure of camp begins when the camper packs her bag and is off for two unforgettable weeks at Onanda. Camp is packed full of fun and great doings from sun-up to sun-down.

Now this sounds like fun!

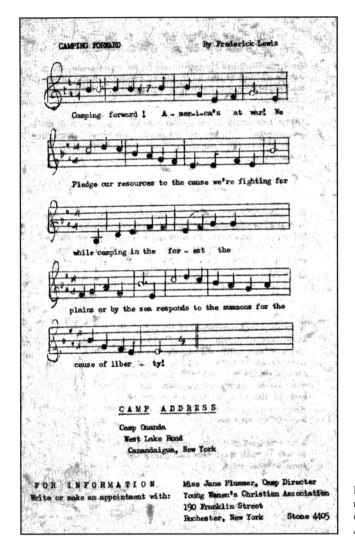

Even camp songs reflected the war. *Courtesy of the Fisher/ Knisley Collection.*

The activities listed had been expanded, too. Camp Crafts, exploring, nature, star hikes, overnights, swimming, boating, tennis, archery, games, simple crafts, ceramics, leatherworking, metalworking, sketching, painting, music, folk dancing, dramatics and Camp Log were on the list.

The mandatory swimming class was in place, keeping everyone mindful of dangers and fun that Canandaigua Lake offered. Boating and craft classes were also consistently offered, but new or different class options would arise as the staff changed. The list of classes was missing photography as an option but had new leatherwork and metalwork classes. This just meant that they were unable to find a counselor able to teach photography but had found gals who could teach leatherwork and metalwork.

While activities came and went, some things at Camp Onanda never changed. After a busy and active day, the girls of Onanda spent evenings together singing and sharing stories around a fire in Crouch Hall or outside under the stars. Evening skits were almost a constant means of sharing the memories that they would carry forever.

Another form of entertainment and lasting memories came from Onanda's neighbors. By the 1940s, Camp Onanda was known by the local boys as the "Girl's Camp." Boys, of course, will be boys, and that means raiding the girl's camp. Ross Anderson's parents had bought the Nest, one of the first rental homes that the YWCA had used, only a few doors south of camp. The Anderson family spent summers there. As a young boy, Ross will now confess, he was a dedicated raider of Camp Onanda. No, he did not raid alone but has kept the identity of the other "lads" unspoken. He shared his youthful adventures as follows:

> *Our raids occurred in the forties. They would normally end with ringing the Camp Onanda bell which told the campers they had been raided. The raids actually would start around dusk when all the children were in Crouch having their evening activities. We would enter the large building that was basically a dorm. That building used to be down by the shore. We'd climb up on the dividing wall in the center and reach up and unscrew the light bulbs until they went out. We would also take towels and tie them together and haul them up the flagpole. We would then quietly depart and would ring the camp bell as we left. The campers would cheer when they knew that they'd been raided for it meant that would stay up later than normal with the maintenance people getting the lights lit.*

Raids were a constant and most often a harmless event of a summer session at Onanda. They would continue throughout the years ahead and be as fondly recalled by campers as they were by the raiders.

By 1948, the cost for camp was now twenty dollars a week with still only a two-dollar registration fee. So a two-week session at Onanda was forty-two dollars for residents of Monroe County and forty-five for girls outside Monroe County. Each session, the one-week high school girls or two-week session for younger girls could accommodate one hundred girls. This meant that four hundred girls could experience Camp Onanda that year without bringing a half a pound of sugar for each week or a ration book of any number.

As the decade of the '40s came to an end, Camp Onanda had returned to carefree days of adventure. Yes, happier days had returned again to Camp Onanda. Rationing was over, and programs were expanded. Yet softly heard—when listening really, really closely—was grumbling from the high school girls. Softly but insistently, they grumbled, "We want more time at camp. We want more time at camp." These girls who had spent many wonderful summers at Onanda when younger were now often turned away for lack of space now that they were teens. A one-week option for high school senior campers was simply not fair.

This just had to change.

MAJOR CHANGES COME TO ONANDA

1950s

As the '50s began, Harry S. Truman was president, the Korean War started and about 4.4 million families in the United States owned a television. There were only forty-eight states, but as the decade ended, two more stars were added to the flag as Alaska and Hawaii become states in January and August 1959, respectively. Eddie Fisher, Perry Como, Dinah Shore and Patti Page crooned their classic pop as the decade began, but Fats Domino, Bo Diddley, Buddy Holly, Brenda Lee, Connie Frances and, of course, Elvis Presley soon took over the radio waves with rock-and-roll. The cold war with the Soviet Union drew Senator McCarthy to radically extend the red scare—making many believe that anyone and everyone was a communist. The Soviet Union successfully launched the space race by being the first to put a satellite into orbit around the earth. Sputnik 1 was not ignored by the United States, as NASA was formed and financed to catch up and get ahead of the Soviet space program.

The 1950s, for most Americans, was a conservative time when family was the focus and just about everyone knew about Mickey Mantle, *I Love Lucy*, *American Bandstand*, Barbie dolls, Davy Crockett, drive-in movies and diners, peddle pushers, 45s (records) and hula hoops. As the '50s came to a close, Dwight D. Eisenhower had been president for seven years, the Vietnam War was beginning and the cold war remained.

The summer of 1950 found Camp Onanda functioning like well-greased gears. Trunks, along with victrolas and radios, were still not allowed at camp, but girls (still mostly from Monroe and Ontario Counties) were filling each session, eager to engage in outdoor activities. For the girls of Monroe County, the cost of a two-week session at camp was forty dollars and those outside the county or state paid forty-three dollars. One two-week session (either the first or last of four scheduled sessions) was for teens only, girls in eighth through twelfth grades. All other sessions were for girls in fourth to eighth grades. Eighth graders had the best of choices in the early '50s, but that, too, would change.

While campers were no longer coming to camp by steamboat or motorboat, they very well may have come by bus. The bus would drop them off in Canandaigua, and the camp station wagon would be there waiting for them. Otherwise, most girls arrived by car with their parents.

The camp no longer provided sheets and pillowcases, but on each bunk, one blanket and pillow were still waiting for campers. Suitcases were filled with suggested items and personal needs. White shorts and shirts were Sunday attire; whatever felt comfortable and practical was suggested for daily wear. Raincoats, along with rubbers or boots, were mentioned, but it's doubtful that rubbers were packed by very many. Returning campers knew a light jacket did the trick and rubbers or boots were just a tad too cautious for a seasoned camper of the '50s. So many of the girls were returning campers in this decade that they likely didn't take the suggested list of what to bring all that seriously.

Dirty clothes could be mailed home, but that too seems unlikely. Girls at summer camp just didn't have the time to wash clothes or even think about mailing dirty clothes home. It's more likely that a few things were washed in sinks, and dirty clothes went home when campers went home.

It almost seems that the YWCA could have charged much more for a session at camp as it almost always had quite a large waiting list. Enough girls were being turned away to fill an entire session and then some. But because the YWCA was committed to providing activities for girls from all walks of life, it kept costs within reach of most working families. About the only thing it could do to shorten that waiting list was to magically expand the camp.

Frankly, little had changed in terms of buildings and space at camp since the late '30s. The original property comprised about twenty-seven acres of land, of which only twelve and a half acres were used well because the balance of the land was largely the steep-sided, wet glen. The twelve and a half acres that included all the buildings and recreational open areas along the lake side of the road hadn't changed all that much since Crouch Hall was dedicated in 1938. The buildings besides Crouch were: Cottage, a nice but smaller cabin that could sleep maybe ten but was used as an infirmary; Wacona, a larger cabin for twenty campers; Abode, once used, years ago, as an overnight cabin for married couples, was now a place for counselors to gather for breaks between classes; Hill House, the Foster home, served as the dining building, camp office and rooms for staff; Little House, the camp director's cabin; Wayside, the caretaker's home across the glen; Babcock Hall, camper's accommodations on the lakefront; a garage; and tool sheds. The fourteen additional acres—including the glen, caretaker's home and some land across the road—had an Adirondack shelter and hiking trails but little more.

While the younger girls, or Junior Campers, had many options for attending camp, the teens had just two choices. They could come for one week at the very beginning of the summer or for one week at the end of the summer. This, according to the teens, was plainly not fair. They talked about this unreasonable situation among themselves and grumbled loudly to adults. And as always happens, when Camp Onanda girls call, someone is listening.

In 1954, the association was able to purchase an additional forty-five acres of land from the Domm family that would extend the camp across West Lake Road, abut the glen and reach high up the hill. Though it would be surrounded by Camp Onanda, the Domm's kept their family home, and about two and a half acres nestled on the west side of the road.

With this additional land purchase, the YWCA of Rochester started its study of modernization for Camp Onanda. As 1955 was ushered in, serious meetings and gatherings and discussion and studies had been long underway. Board members, trustees, present and former camp directors and camp consultants all came to the conclusion that the estimated funds needed to modernize and truly put all Onanda's land to use was $234,900.

Whoa! Now that's a lot of money. In 1955, the average cost of building a three-bedroom home was about $5,000. Where would the money needed, come from?

The largest campaign for modernizing and enlarging Onanda was begun.

In 1955, the YWCA of the United States was celebrating one hundred years of service to women. This was a great time for the Rochester YWCA to begin its building finance drive for Camp Onanda because the national association promised more than $30,000 to the Rochester association specifically for the camp.

Another major assistance in planning came from the American Camping Association (ACA). The ACA believed that decentralizing units—cabins for

Right: Remodeling at last. *Courtesy of the University of Rochester.*

Below: The plans for Teen Hill. *Courtesy of the University of Rochester.*

eight to ten campers with required counselors—provided a safer and more enriching camping experience. It encouraged the YWCA to eliminate the huge housing (Babcock Hall).

Initially, thoughts were that Babcock Hall would be modernized. Instead, it was decided that Babcock would be cut apart and moved to different locations. One large wing of Babcock would remain on the waterfront and act as a boathouse and craft area. The other large wing of Babcock would be moved up parallel to West Lake Road and serve as a dining hall for the entire camp. The middle section of Babcock, that Alpine-looking center, was not mentioned in the original modernization proposal but it, too, was salvaged and became Heaho, a cabin for campers. Wacona, the large, long building would be partitioned off into four separate areas that would accommodate eight to ten campers each. Cottage would become Soyowase, another cabin for ten or more campers. Eventually, Hill House, no longer needed for dining, would become the camp office, a residence for some staff and the camp infirmary. The two dining areas on either side of Hill House would be converted into separate sleeping areas for two groups of eight to ten campers. Finally, two new cabins would be added to the waterfront side of camp near the boathouse. A larger, vastly improved washhouse and a smaller washhouse would end up composing Lower Camp.

This doesn't even address the new, forty-seven acres of land across the road. The initial proposal for the new hill property was to build ten new cabins for the teenage campers, two washhouses and a lodge. The lodge would be used on rainy days and for evening activities.

If this proposal succeeded, there would be ten camper cabins on Lower Camp and ten more on the hill.

A huge, multi-folded and tri-colored brochure was printed and distributed to those whom the association hoped would be major financial contributors. There were diagrams of the new buildings wanted, pictures of past summer sessions and a lengthy report of how the costs were determined.

The chapters of the association didn't drag their feet either—baked food sales, raffles, every kind of fundraising project was put into motion.

Up until now, Babcock Hall and Wacona accommodated one hundred campers, tops. This new plan would accommodate from eighty to one hundred campers on the lakefront side of camp and add the same number of campers to the newly purchased land. Onanda would double in the number of girls that could come to camp, which, of course, meant that the older teens would have all the same session options that the younger girls had. At least, that was hope.

This was part of the YWCA's presentation:

It is proposed to decentralize the residence units for campers. At present there is a dormitory arrangement with 80 campers in one large frame building. This does not provide a typically outdoor camping experience, rather a resort type atmosphere. It makes supervision difficult and constitutes some definite hazards.

Oddly, it seems, Babcock Hall was now a hazard. Well, this was a plea for money, and like all negotiating, painting a "needy" picture got better results. Babcock likely did need some major upgrades and structural fixing up after more than thirty years of use. So the YWCA went with the ACA's suggestion of putting girls of the same age in smaller groups with counselors. This truly would be safer and would provide a more meaningful experience. Ten units for younger girls would be on Lower Camp, and the teenagers would have ten new cabins on the new property across the lake road.

Also noted in the presentation was that the new cabins to be built would cost no more than a garage to construct. That would likely mean a cost somewhere in the neighborhood of $400 a cabin. Of course, that's just material costs. Building ten cabins, two washhouses and a lodge on a hillside is far more challenging than paper plans indicated.

Still, it was to be a tough sell, and it took nearly two years to get hammers and saws humming again at Camp Onanda. The exact amount raised is not known, but the 1957 brochure proudly and excitedly announced that the modernization of Lower Camp was completed and "greater use will be made of the newly acquired camping area." That "newly acquired" area would be Teen Town.

Junior campers marveled at the newness of Onanda in 1957 and jumped right into activities. Teen campers were still waiting for Teen Town to be completed. While that must have seemed an agonizing wait, Teen Town emerged slowly from the hillside.

In the summer of 1958, Teen Town consisted of three cabins; King Hall, for teen gatherings; and a large washhouse ready and open for business. The cabin design was changed from the brochure design, and one very large washhouse rather than two was another change made to the original plan. Still, a spanking-new area for teens was taking form on Teen Hill. That would be the first summer that junior campers and teens would share Onanda all summer.

As the last camper and staff left Onanda in the summer of 1958, the workers returned. Carpenters, volunteers and anyone able to assist headed up that steep, dirt road to Teen Town, bent on the goal of completing the modernization plan set forth three years earlier. That meant getting the foundations set for seven more cabins on a steep hillside, carting materials up that steep incline and doing it within a couple months before winter set in and finishing work in the spring.

It's just not known for sure how this new teen area of camp was renamed. Maybe the change came from builders who must have carried materials up and down that hill. Then, too, the girls of summer who would hike up and down that hill many times a day may have renamed it. Even though the YWCA maps of Onanda always designated this new area as Teen Town, campers and staff always called it Teen Hill.

What is known is that every cabin on Camp Onanda now had a name and identity that would never change. The Lower Camp cabins were Wapoos (rabbit), Tilipe (fox), Anekul (squirrel), Wequash (swan), Soyowase (bear), Skajuna (eagle), Hayowentha (turtle), Wikis (bird), Wapagokhas (owl) and Heaho (deer). Teen Hill cabins were Kiniks (rosebud), Adsila (flower), Tona (turkey), Litahni (flame), Wahihi (snowflake), Chule (tree), Soyazhe (star), Namid (dancer), Chowat (girl) and Oawensa (sunflower). The boathouse was named Gaowo (canoe) and Hill House was dubbed Haudenosaunee (hill people) but were always referred to as the boathouse and Hill House.

Rochester YWCA

Camp Onanda

WEST LAKE ROAD

CANANDAIGUA, NEW YORK

The new and improved Camp Onanda. *Courtesy of the Fisher/Knisley Collection.*

Onanda's thirty-forth season, 1959, welcomed girls in fourth to twelfth grades to choose which of the four two-week sessions they would come to camp. Teen Town was completed!

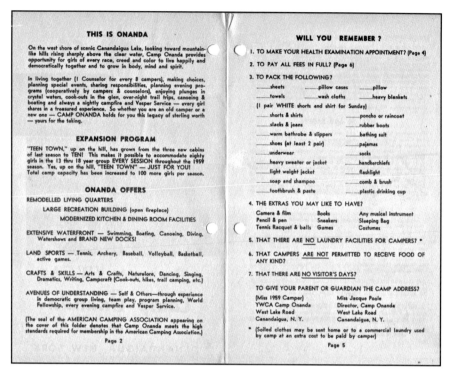

The expansion program completed. *Courtesy of the Fisher/Knisley Collection.*

Ten nicely spacious cabins, scattered across the hillside with magnificent views of the lake below, would be filled to capacity every session. The teenagers' call had been answered.

While it might seem that Onanda was now two separate camps, it was not. It was now a seventy-and-a-half-acre camp that grouped campers in twenty cabins by age. All meals were shared together and free time activities were often shared. There were all-camp cookouts on the beach and all-camp special events. While housed in separate areas and generally having evening campfires separately, there was always a magical bond between the girls of Lower Camp and Teen Hill, making Onanda one great camp for girls.

A typical day at camp for a teen involved three classes after breakfast that were held on Lower Camp. Campers chose their classes for the session. Swimming, which required class no matter what level of ability, was one of the classes. There was free swim before lunch. After lunch, the teens would hike up the hill for rest hour and then cabin activities. Cabin activities varied, and sometimes one cabin joined with another. Before supper, a second free swim was offered. After supper, there was one more class and then campfire and bed. For Lower Camp campers, the activities were in reverse until supper. They would have their cabin activities in the morning, and the bulk of their classes in the afternoon.

Most classes were held on Lower Camp. The waterfront, archery field, play fields, tennis courts and Crouch Hall were in a constant state of activity every single day.

Let us here describe the hike to and from those new Teen Hill cabins. No, the girls did not cross West Lake Road coming from or going to Teen Hill. It was simply not allowed. There was no bridge over the road either. So how did they manage that?

Well, West Lake Road, a mere fifteen or so feet south of the gate into Lower Camp, had a small bridge over Onanda's glen. The girls simply went under that bridge, remaining safe and virtually unseen by drivers.

Coming out from under the bridge and up from the glen, the "hike" truly began. A steep, rugged dirt and shale road, first used by those who built Teen Town, wound slightly up the wooded hill along the north edge of the glen. About five minutes into the hike, when one's breath was near gasping, the road turned to the right, trees melted away and the huge open hillside appeared. Farther up were the ten nicely positioned Teen Hill cabins and huge washhouse.

If you were fortunate enough to be assigned to Kiniks, your hike ended first. For others, there was a fair amount of climbing yet to conquer.

No more grumbling came from teenaged girls for more time at camp, but often, with light-hearted tones, one might pick up grumbles from someone who had arrived on Lower Camp only to realized she forgotten something up in her cabin.

It must be mentioned that Camp Onanda was blessed to have consistent leadership who championed the camp at the Rochester YWCA during the decades of the '50s and '60s. These folks didn't view summer camp as a luxury but rather a commitment to providing for girls of all ages.

At the close of this decade, Camp Onanda was fully modernized and accommodated two hundred campers and counselors each session, as well as a small overflow if needed. The grounds and buildings were clearly defined and, for now, only required regular care. Not until the early '70s would additional and major modernization come.

BLASTING INTO THE '60S

The 1960s brought the first televised presidential debates. The Berlin Wall was built, Adolf Eichmann was on trial for his role in the Holocaust and U.S. troops were being sent to Vietnam. Medgar Evers, John F. Kennedy, Malcolm X, Martin Luther King Jr. and Robert F. Kennedy were assassinated. Neil Armstrong became the first man to land on the moon, and the Beatles landed in the U.S. music world. Tie-dye T-shirts, long hair and Andy Warhol's Campbell Soup Cans were totally "far out." Believe it or not, the first Super Bowl was played in 1967. To call someone an "aardvark" was an endearing tease. The '60s were unsettling and tearful times mixed with great achievements. As Neil Armstrong stepped onto the moon, Camp Onanda was celebrating its fiftieth birthday, and radios were still not allowed at camp.

When Camp Onanda gives her call,
We'll answer campers, one and all,
Oo-N-A-N-D-Aa, Onanda,
Oo-N-A-N-D-Aa, Onanda!

Nearly every summer's night in the '60s, this musical round floated across the water of Canandaigua Lake and across Teen Hill. Nightly, the bursts from crackling fires on the shore and hillside, girls giggling as skits unfolded and camp songs being sung were heard. Bug juice (a concoction similar to Cool-Aid) and marshmallows for roasting or making s'mores were common campfire treats. The lapping of the lake on the shore near Lower Camp's campfire circle and the sounds of the woods around Teen Hill's fire gently announced the end of a day at Onanda in the '60s.

As with previous decades, girls came to Onanda from far and wide. Most of the campers were from the Rochester and Canandaigua areas, but other counties and states were represented, too. Some counselors came from Florida, Pennsylvania, Georgia, Texas, Oklahoma and even as far away as Finland and Sweden, but the majority of the staff were New York State natives.

While any girl who experienced Camp Onanda will likely tell you that the summers she spent there were the best years, it must be said that the decade of the '60s was truly exceptional. The camp was so entirely well established and the leadership so strong that it was nearly impossible that any girl wanted to go home after a two- or four-week stay.

The draw of Onanda was always very apparent the first day of every session. It would be a Sunday afternoon. The staff would have hustled about in the morning preparing last-minute things and getting settled into their assigned

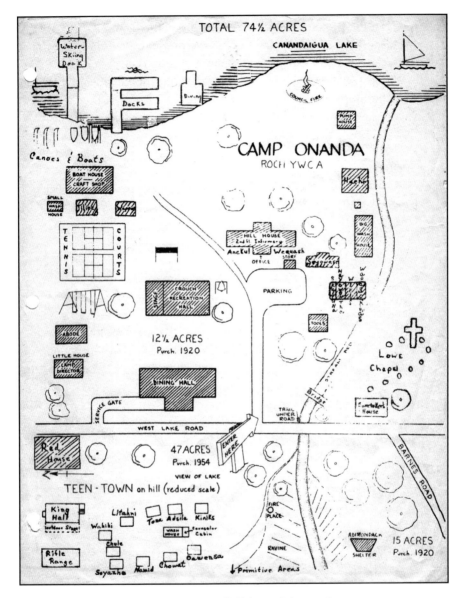

Teen Town/Teen Hill on the map. *From the YWCA counselor's manual.*

cabin. Around 10:30 a.m., the gate to camp would be closed. Closed, you wonder? Yes, it was closed because even though the arrival hours were clearly designated as 2:00 p.m. to 4:00 p.m., by the time the staff headed to their last lunch without campers, cars were lined up for at least a mile down the West Lake Road filled with eager campers and their families.

YWCA Camp Onanda, in the 1960s, included the Domm house and two acres that the Domm family had kept in the original purchase of the Teen Hill property. Divided by West Lake Road, the seventy-four and a half acres of the Camp Onanda were cared for year-round by Charlie Metz in the early '60s and then by Arnold Smeenk from 1964 to '75. These men were dedicated caretakers and men of nature. The care they invested into every corner of camp was more than apparent the minute you stepped onto the land. Their job was enormous, and they met every challenge with genuine respect and unending skill.

Surely you can imagine the issues that arise when two hundred girls invaded the camp. But it didn't end with eight weeks of constant use. This was a year-round job, as the camp was rented out to other groups prior to and after Camp Onanda's regular season. Even in winter, some groups used the camp. Likely the only calm and quiet the keepers of Onanda knew came for a couple weeks in February.

By the time the staff arrived for a week of Pre-Camp indoctrination, everything was in order.

Pre-Camp was a hectic time. Forty-five girls, several not much older than the eldest campers but mostly college students, would spend the week learning the ways and laws of camp. They were on a tight schedule of meetings and working out the final touches on the areas they would be teaching. Camp songs were learned around campfires in the evening, drills for emergency situations were practiced, Special Event Days were decided on, and staff show crews were selected. Paddles, oars, boats and sails were checked for safety and readiness. Supplies were inventoried and renewed for non-waterfront classes. All things that made for a successful camp were fully addressed. By the end of the week, the entire staff of fifty plus knew what was expected of them as staff, and they knew one another as well.

While Pre-Camp was primarily a serious time of learning and preparation, it was also a time for simply enjoying the activities that campers would soon have. Counselors found time for hikes and waterskiing, sailing and canoeing, pulling pranks and even a visit to town one evening. It was often during Pre-Camp that counselors "found" their camp name. Susan, the waterfront director, would be Splash. Martha, from the Lone Star State, would, of course, be Tex. For a variety of reasons, names like Cap, Peaches, Hilly, Twinkles, Apples, Bugsy, Putt, Flash, Mouse, Okie, Limpy and Cookie were adopted for summer camp.

Two counselors were assigned to each of the twenty cabins. After four weeks (two camp sessions), counselors were reassigned. This allowed counselors to work with different age groups and different counselors. Lower Camp cabins varied in size and appearance while the Teen Hill cabins were pretty much the same, having all been built at the same period of time. Teen Hill cabins were not quite as wide as a detached, single-car garage but were about four feet longer. Though a tight fit for eight to ten campers and two counselors, no complaints were heard. Heaho and Soyawase in Lower Camp were the largest, somewhat desired cabins. Heaho was nearly two stories tall, as it had been the center portion of the old Babcock Hall. Soyawase had served as an infirmary and was divided into three sections. Campers slept on either end and the counselors in the middle.

The girls of Camp Onanda obviously made close ties with their cabin mates. A typical Teen Hill cabin held five or six metal bunk beds, two single beds for counselors and had just about enough room for suitcases and trunks. The windows were screened (no glass). To keep out rain or ward off chilly nights, the outer shutters were closed. Three open light bulbs attached to the rafters provided light when needed. Rustic could describe the cabin, and close quarters were the norm. But this rustic closeness fostered the formation of lifelong memories and friendships.

Try to remember when you were eight or nine years old. In order to enter the dining hall for lunch, you must write a postcard or letter home. Your counselor has gently suggested that you need to write only a sentence or two about your first week at camp but to make sure to include the cabin name. Sounds easy enough, unless you happen to be in Wapagokhas. At nine years old, the spelling of your cabin's name is challenging, and postcard space is small. Even so, you squeezed it all in because you want to eat, and that long, funny name has become your identity at Onanda.

Kammy M. hailed from Elmira, New York, Hilary G. from Rochester. The summer of 1963 found them in the same Lower Camp cabin for their first two-week adventure at Camp Onanda. Little did these eleven-year-olds know, as their parents helped them settle into Wapoos that last session of '63, a forever friendship was about to begin, as well as a never-ending connection with Onanda. Kammy and Hilary would totally absorb all things Onanda that first summer. Everything was new and fun, and the two weeks seemed to fly by in a blur. As they returned summer after summer, they eagerly awaited favorite activities and got excited about the new ones they'd explore.

What was it about this place that kept bringing girls back year after year or, in Kammy's and Hilary's cases, for a decade plus of summers?

Friendships forged in shared experiences were likely the foremost reason for returning. Then, too, there were simply so many experiences to be had that no one could possibly include them all in one summer. No session was ever the same, and somehow campers found out what happened at Camp Onanda even when they weren't there. They would hear about a special activity that they missed, like the Fourth of July fireworks. The entire camp, in shifts, would be bused to the town of Cheshire to enjoy the display. Obviously, you had to be at camp on the Fourth of July.

Girls came back to camp year after year for as many reasons as there were adventures to be had.

Special Event Days and activities were incorporated into a tight, two-week schedule. Four-week campers and the rare eight-week campers never experienced the same Special Event Day during their stay at Onanda. On these special themed days, there were no classes. Instead, the entire camp would be transformed. Lower Camp might become a carnival site with a parade and booths or a huge arena for an Olympics Day for which any number of challenging contests were held.

How many girls don't like horses? Around 1962, horseback riding was offered at camp for an additional fee. If you signed up for a "riding cabin," off you would go to the Double Diamond Ranch. This meant a bus ride on the "Dust Bowl Express." The most direct route to the Double Diamond Ranch from camp was mostly on dirt and gravel roads. With at least one other cabin and one of your cabin counselors, you would ride up, around and down Bristol Mountain. Just listening to Mel's stories (the owner of the ranch) as the horses were saddled-up made for one of those rare experiences of summer camp.

Camp Onanda's waterfront offered up so many choices it would make your head spin! Of course, some classes and free-time activities were dependent on swimming ability, but Red Cross–certified classes were provided. As a camper successfully completed a better swimming level, she had more waterfront choices. Dependent on one's swimming ability, those choices included boating (rowboat), canoeing, sailing, water skiing, synchronized swimming, lifesaving or diving. There was Polar Bear Club for those brave enough to take an early morning, almost always cold, swim before breakfast. A free swim before lunch and again before dinner might include a rousing game of water volleyball or a quick sail on the Sailfish. Fishing was not discouraged, but the constant, almost always loud and rowdy use of the waterfront did not make for an ideal fishing atmosphere.

Choices for land classes were just as exciting and varied. Arts and crafts projects changed from session to session and year to year. In Camp Crafts, girls learned such things as how to make a proper fire from scratch and how to build things from only items found in nature. There were classes in archery, music and dance, writing, tennis, nature studies, first aid, hiking and orienteering and even rifelry for Teen Hill girls. Any activity you could imagine at summer camp, Onanda offered.

Once each session, always on a Saturday, a Teen Hill cabin was paired with a Lower Camp cabin for an all-camp cookout on the beach. Counselors fondly, or not so fondly, referred to this as the All-Camp Grease Out. In the morning, the Lower Camp cabin would choose a spot on the shore to set up the evening cooking fire. They would gather wood for the fire, dig a fire pit and set the wood in place. The Teen Hill cabin would later light the fire and cook the meal. Both cabins cleaned up the fire pits and any messes after the shared meal. While a great uniting activity for the girls, after a busy day of activities, this was not the sort of thing counselors truly enjoyed. It did, however, definitely give everyone a greater appreciation for those who cooked three meals a day for the camp.

Cabin Camping, that two and half hour block of time for each cabin to pursue whatever activity or adventure they wanted, was often planned on the spur of the moment. Weather often dictated the direction a cabin would take. However, no matter what the weather, Cabin Camping was about memories made as a cabin.

Following lunch each day was "rest hour." After getting the day's mail and maybe stopping by the camp store, campers and counselors gathered in their cabins, but rest was rarely the norm. Though confined to the cabin, this was time to share what had unfolded during the morning, write a note home or to a friend, plan for an overnight away from camp or prepare for leading a campfire or a flag raising or lowering. It was a quieter time but rarely truly restful.

While special activities were abundant, one Teen Hill–only event was always highly looked forward to: the Camp Cory/Camp Onanda exchange dance. Camp Cory, a YMCA camp (as in Young *Men's* Christian Association) was on Keuka Lake, the Finger Lake just east of Canandaigua. Each summer, Camp Cory and then Camp Onanda hosted this dance, so the campers got two dances per summer. When the dance was at Camp Cory, the Onanda girls piled into the camp bus for the thirty-minute ride. When it was at Onanda, the girls decorated Crouch Hall for the exciting evening. The kitchen staff rounded up snacks and bug juice. All had a great time. The Cory/Onanda dances ceased around 1976, when Camp Cory went co-ed.

As darkness fell on Onanda after a busy and exhausting day, campers and staff headed for their campfires. Each night, a different cabin planned what songs would be sung, what snacks would be shared and some kind of entertainment. The planned "entertainment" might be that a bag held the names of every counselor at camp. Each cabin would pull a name from the bag and keep that name a secret. The mission of the cabin would be to come up with ten adjectives that would describe that counselor but not include her name. The adjectives were clues for the other cabins to use to guess who the counselor was. The cabin that used the fewest adjectives before the correct counselor was identified would win some prize or extra snack. The cabins that failed to get their person identified might have an additional task or booby prize. On Lower Camp or Teen Hill, campfires were filled with laughter, songs and snacks. The songs sung around those campfires were often the same and are easily recalled by former campers and staff.

One activity was truly rare and never forgotten, *if* your cabin could schedule it and *if* the weather cooperated. Along the southern property line of Onanda is a glorious glen, sometimes referred to as Barnes Glen. Every cabin almost always accomplished a hike up the glen. After about a twenty-minute hike into this incredible gift of nature, the first of three waterfall areas was reached. If enough water was flowing, it was glen-sliding day! You definitely needed to wear an old pair of shorts that could be tossed

Glen sliding. *Courtesy of the Fisher/Knisley Collection.*

away because sliding down Mother Nature's water slide meant destroyed shorts. Girls scaled up the dry side of the falls, sidled across the flat landing about midway up the water flow and then simply sat down and pushed off! Though girls went home with one pair of shorts totally beyond repair, it was so worth the loss of a pair of shorts.

The first Sunday of each two-week session was Special Events Day. Again, no theme was the same, and the entire camp was involved. Each cabin dressed in outfits that fit the theme of the day and had something to contribute to the day's activities. Meals were held as usual, but nothing else was usual about the day. It was just a day of creative and fun activities.

On Sundays, there were no classes. Before the special events began, all at Onanda put on their Sunday best, green shorts and a white blouse, for an outdoor chapel service, most often organized by the CITs (counselors in training). The entire camp gathered in Lowe Chapel to give thanks for all things. Imagine "church" outside in nature! It was the perfect setting. Then, too, accommodations were made for the Roman Catholic girls to attend church in town. Always, respect was given to Sundays.

Several Camp Onanda traditions unfolded at the close of every two-week session.

At some point during the last two days of a session, each cabin group received its "last will and testament" from its cabin counselors. Each camper was "memorialized" with some silly "gift" that reflected something accomplished or done to make that cabin experience fun. Bequeathing an alarm clock that forever goes off at six o'clock in the morning might be for the camper who had a hard time getting up mornings. Only the cabin would know the reason for each bequest. All was in fun and just a personal recognition of each camper.

The second to last night of the two-week session was Awards Night. At an extended dinner, campers were presented awards, and the Outstanding Campers were announced and given a special sailboat charm for a bracelet or necklace. No evening classes were held because dinner ran long and then everyone went to Crouch Hall for the Camper Talent Show.

Every cabin, from both Lower Camp and Teen Hill, would present a skit, sing a song or share some talent in an evening show that went on until it was finished. The stage was decked out with a backdrop made by the campers. Counselors roared at imitations of themselves or got misty-eyed listening to songs and stories of the two weeks that had just unfolded. Needless to say, it was an evening of laughter and reflection.

The last night at camp was always a late and emotional one. After a day of final activities, the entire staff put on a show for the campers. Very much

The campers' talent show. *Courtesy of Nancy Showalter-Clark.*

as the campers had done the evening before, the staff put on skits, sang songs and simply shared their fond memories of the session. Shows always had some sort of theme, and backdrops were truly incredible, but it was the sharing that kept every camper wide-eyed and content.

Immediately following the staff show was the emotional and meaningful Wish Boat Ceremony. At some point during the day, each camper had made a wish boat. A wish boat was a small paper plate on which the camper had written a wish or camp memory. Wish boats were decorated and then a candle was secured to each one. The entire camp would arrive at the waterfront, wish boats in hand, to find a huge fire already dancing in the night. Several soft and moving camp songs were sung as each girl went to the water's edge,

The staff show. *Courtesy of Nancy Showalter-Clark.*

lit the candle of her wish boat and then placed it on the water. After the last wish boat set sail, everyone, almost silently but often tearfully, headed to their cabins. Summer camp had come to an end for these two-week campers.

It is important to mention that Mother Nature was not angry with paper plates floating on her waters. In the lake were several counselors who gathered up the plates as they rounded the point beyond the view of the campers.

It was events like these that surely had girls pestering their parents for time at Camp Onanda. Parents must have been pleased to oblige, as every session of the '60s had a waiting list.

Now, you might be pondering if a day at Camp Onanda could really be so full and flow so well with over two hundred girls in the mix. Ponder no longer! Come along for a morning with Oawensa, the cabin highest up Teen Hill.

Rise and Shine in the '60s!

It's seven o'clock in the morning. Ready or not, the day begins with a rousing rendition of "Reveille" from the rarely used speaker system. The speaker

86

system is used sparingly so as not to offend or annoy neighbors of the camp, but it is a necessity to get the day started, especially for the girls way up on Teen Hill. Get up! Get moving!

Now, maybe you're among a few gals who would have risen before "Reveille" sounded and headed to the waterfront for the Polar Bear Club. Yes, this was an early morning dip in Canandaigua's invigorating water. As you can imagine, participation in the Polar Bear Club is not huge. To earn official membership, you have to make this early morning swim several morningss during the next two weeks. Not many managed this feat. Will you?

Some of your cabin mates popped from bed and headed to the washhouse while others needed a little coaxing. Beds must be made and cabins straightened for the daily inspection by the camp nurse. Yes, for those who

No cleanliness award here. *Courtesy of Nancy Showalter-Clark.*

maintain their cabin well, a cleanliness award will be given at the end of the session, so there is some incentive to keep a cabin tidy. With eight to ten campers and two counselors in each cabin, cleanliness is not as easy as it sounds.

Grab your towel, swimsuit and whatever you need for classes because you do not want to climb back up the hill. You need to get to the flag raising! Your counselor reminds you how lucky it is that the cabin doesn't have to set tables for breakfast since you're running a little slow.

The entire camp population is gathered around the flagpole. Heaho is doing the flag raising today. Donning the sashes of flag color guards, Heaho marches down the slope from Hill House in smart formation with a properly folded flag. In unison, the girls halt about ten feet from the flagpole. The gal with the flag and two others step away and to the pole. The flag is securely clipped, and again, the speaker system plays a military, flag-raising bugle song as the flag is hoisted. Campers and counselors stand respectfully quiet until the flag is up, and Heaho marches smartly back to Hill House.

With campers, counselors and flag up, it's time for breakfast! Can you even fathom attempting to feed 250 people at the same time? It happened at Onanda with seeming ease. Gert McCormick, Carol Phelps and Millie Burd were three incredible ladies who not only "handled" all preparations, but also did it with smiles and provided fabulous meals. These ladies were fully a major part of everything Onanda.

You run to the boathouse with some cabin mates to leave your things and then run back up to the dinning hall and get in line with everyone else who is waiting. The CITs are essentially holding off the flood of hungry people until things are ready inside and encouraging a morning song. Finally, all is ready, and in you pour.

At the beginning of camp, your cabin was assigned a table where you sit for every meal, so you know exactly where to go. As you sit down, your counselor picks the two "hoppers" for breakfast. You're one of them. Hoppers have to "hop" up to the kitchen counter and bring the family-style dishes of food, pitchers of juice and milk and, for that matter, anything else needed to the table.

Before hoppers hopped or food was set out, everyone sang grace. You sang right along.

Oh the Lord is good to me, and so I thank the Lord,
For giving me the things I need,
The birds and bees and the appleseed,
The Lord is good me.

Anyone, any cabin, late for a meal has to sing grace in front of those already seated. That embarrassment is avoided at all cost. But the entire Tona cabin was late, so their day started in the spotlight.

Just to tease you some, your counselor makes a request for something each time you go to sit. Having hoppers makes for less confusion, as the hoppers are the only ones out of their seats during a meal. Sometimes a hopper's food gets cool with all their hopping for others.

No, meals are not quiet, but they are not without manners either. One might hear a table erupt into song, "Mary, Mary strong and able / Keep your elbows off the table"—another embarrassment to be avoided. But meals are meant to be enjoyed and that includes good manners.

Though you're hustling around, you heard Elise talking about how this was going to be a great day because she has a sailing class and she will man the tiller. Beth and Gail are a little nervous about Camp Crafts because they're doing lashing and they're not sure they really understand how to do it. The dinning hall is abuzz with relatively quiet chatter, and it dawns on you as you dig into your now semi-cold eggs: you have a swimming test today.

Just as you're about finished eating, the camp director gets up and says she has a couple announcements. Before she can say another word, the entire dinning hall bursts into song.

> *Announcements, Announcements, A-now-ounce-ments!*
> *What a horrible way to die, what a horrible way to die,*
> *What a horrible way to be talked to death what a horrible way to die.*
> *Announcements, Announcements, A-now-ounce-ments!*

With a slight roll of her eyes and a hint of a smile, Skip reminds everyone that it's a horseback riding day, and riders must be on time. She has a sweatshirt that someone might be looking for and there will be zebra cake at supper tonight. Someone from Tilipe grabs the sweatshirt as cheers erupt over zebra cake.

You take your dishes and silverware up to the proper containers and notice that your cabin is still sitting at the table as others are slowly leaving. When you get back to the table, Anne reminds you that the cabin has cleanup. That means thoroughly washing all the tables down and sweeping the entire dinning hall. It will be a mad rush to class.

With the dinning hall cleaned, you are now running at top speed for the waterfront because the bell has rung and that means class will begin in five minutes. Luckily, you have advanced canoeing first and don't need to change into a swimsuit. All you need to do is grab a paddle and lifejacket from the boathouse and scoot down the shore to the canoes. You can do this.

You actually skid across the shale beach and arrive to class on time only to learn that you need to go back and get into your swimsuit. Twinkles explains that you must have forgotten that today you are going to purposely tip over your canoe so you can learn to right it and get back in.

It's not even nine o'clock yet. It feels much later.

Rather than use a speaker system too often, the bell signaled all things important during the day. The bell is your friend—and your enemy, if you are lagging. It rings for classes. It rings for free swims. It rings for meals. It keeps everyone aware of the transitions needed to keep a flow to the day.

You've just learned that righting a swamped canoe is not too hard but getting back into it is something entirely different. The bell has rung, and you have five minutes to get to your swimming class. Remember? This is test day. You have to jump into the water fully clothed and make a buoy out of your slack while treading water.

Off you scoot to the boathouse to put on slacks and a blouse over your wet bathing suit. You grab your sneakers too and head for the dock. Shay greets your class with a smile and announces that this is the big day. Dressed like you, she demonstrates the test at hand. She jumps into the lake, talking to the class as she treads water. She first takes off her sneakers, ties them together and puts them around her neck. Then she gets her slacks off and ties knots in each leg. Effortlessly, she drains water from her slacks, whips them over her head and presto! Holding the waistband under the surface of the water, the legs of the slacks are filled with air and hold her up.

About twenty minutes later, you learn that this is not as easy as Shay made it look. Still, you somehow passed the test. You're pleased with your accomplishment, but it's nearly time to get to Camp Crafts.

The bell rings. Off you go! Today, your mission in Camp Crafts is to collect the proper kindling and wood to start a fire. You have to build this in sequence and actually get it burning. Corky has reminded you how important the first layer is to your success and that you will only be given three matches to get your fire started. You gather your materials just fine, but it's windy, causing you to use up your matches. Corky checks your tinder and tells you if she can light it with one match it's well prepared. You hold your breath and…it lights! Now you see how to protect a lighted match from the wind.

You have about ten minutes to douse your fire and clean up the area before free swim. Your swimming buddy will be waiting for you, and you're excited about getting to water ski. Still, you are very careful about completely dousing your fire.

Even though you are skiing, you grab your buddy tag because you're on the waterfront and head for the skiing raft. As you wait your turn, the girls playing water volleyball grab your attention. The Skajuna girls are winning. Suddenly, two sharp blows from a guard's whistle bring silence to the waterfront. Girls grab their buddies' hands and hold them high. Buddy checks are made regularly during every free swim. About forty seconds later, one sharp whistle blows, signaling that all is well. Noise erupts right where it left off.

Tick gave you a longer than usual ski run today because not many signed up. The water was choppier than you're used to, but you didn't fall. As you take off your skis and lifebelt, your legs feel rubbery. Since you were the last skiing run, you really have to hustle to get dressed for lunch. Just as you tie your sneaks, the lunch bell rings. Again, you will be running to be on time, and you're laughing as you notice Elise and Timbi just pulling the Sailfish onto the shore. You know they'll be late and singing grace to the rest of camp.

I'm pretty sure that you now understand that a day at camp is one of constant motion. Sure, there are moments of frustration and grumbling, but by the end of the day, every camper has learned much, laughed often and knows it has been a great day. Sleep will come easily.

While time was tightly structured, campers had a lot of input into the activities. Campers had chosen the classes they participated in that session. They planned campfire programs, their overnight away from camp and daily cabin activities like hikes, glen sliding or just relaxing. If someone in the cabin had a birthday, it was celebrated. Though no radios or televisions were anywhere in camp, let alone "allowed" in camp, girls had absolutely no problem filling their time. Always, more adventures were hoped for than could be fulfilled in one summer at Onanda.

Tools of the Trade and Leadership in the '60s

The success of any organization most definitely is dependent on its leadership. From its very first years, the YWCA of Rochester was truly blessed with incredible camp leaders. Their jobs, in the last four decades of Onanda, were not seasonal either.

The camp director had to know everything about camp, from how many tennis balls there were to what needed repair. They had to be business women, too, knowing exactly how much money was needed for repairs, salaries, replacement costs and the costs of feeding a camper three meals a day. The camp director had to be a teacher, a CEO, a lover of nature, a fund raiser, an advertiser and, above all, a determined but patient person.

Counselors had to be interviewed and certifications checked, especially those seeking waterfront positions. Staff selection was a long and thorough process. Each year, a new camp brochure had to be designed and sent out to former campers and made available to potential campers. A staff manual had to be revised regularly. When other groups rented the camp, the director did the scheduling and oversaw the preparations for each group. As registrations started coming in for the regular Onanda season, the camp director made cabin assignments by age and interests. To simply make repairs at camp meant meetings to get the repair approved; finding the best, most cost-efficient means to make the repair; and being on site as the repair was made. From purchasing new items to adding new activities at camp, nearly every aspect of running a camp meant meetings.

OK, now you're in charge, you're a director, one of the "bosses" for a regular summer session. I bet you're thinking, "This is going to be a lot easier than keeping up with a camper's day." Think again.

You have to be prepared for the recreational needs of 250 girls, every two weeks for two months in 1960. What equipment do you need? What things will likely need to be replaced? How will you distribute and keep track of items? What items, for legal reasons, must be available? How many campers and staff have special needs, and how should you place them? Where will the grounds people and kitchen staff be housed? How will you handle food deliveries? Where does one begin to organize all the aspects of a summer camp? It just isn't as easy as it sounds.

The Onanda of the '60s had a small armada of canoes. Fortunately, aluminum replaced the wood and canvas canoes in popularity, and the YWCA found great merit in aluminum. When camp was in session, the fifteen aluminum canoes were kept on racks on the shoreline. Each canoe was numbered and identified as YWCA property. One enormous wood-and-canvas canoe (called a war canoe, which could easily hold an entire cabin of girls), was also kept on the beach.

Pulled up on the beach and turned bottoms up was a small fleet of rowboats. Eight aluminum rowboats had their YWCA identification as well. Buoyed about twenty feet from shore were *Struggle* and *Success*, two six-seater, fiberglass Javelin sailboats. The names for the sailboats tell the story of how difficult these sailboats were to acquire, not a designation of sailing ability. In the boathouse was stored one fiberglass Sailfish that was only used for free swim sailing. In a boat rack is nestled a powerboat. This was used for water skiing classes and by the directors to check up on cabins that went off in canoes for an overnight. This fleet needed to be constantly checked for safety and compliance with state laws. The motorboat had to be serviced, fueled and licensed.

Maintaining these boats and keeping track of them is a straightforward task, but finding counselors who could teach campers how to safely and responsibly enjoy these boats was another bowl of fish.

To move canoes and rowboats through the water, paddles and oars are a necessity, and in the 1960s, that meant wood. Wood meant carefully watching for cracks and good varnish cover. Girls from nine to seventeen come in all shapes and sizes, so paddles did as well. Paddles were kept in the boathouse, hanging from walls and inspected constantly.

No girl went into a boat of any shape without a life preserver. Not only was it the law, but it was also just good thinking. Another wall of the boathouse held bright orange lifejackets and ski belts of every size. These safety necessities are well used and, being so well used, need replacing every now and then.

You're getting the picture, I'm sure. Whether dealing with land activities or water activities, a summer camp had a huge investment in recreational "tools of the trade." There were tennis rackets and balls, badminton rackets, nets and birdies, croquet mallets, tether balls, softballs, bats, volleyballs, kickballs, bows and arrows, rifles and ammunition, hay bales for targets, rifle range targets and on and on it goes.

If this seems too much to deal with, consider the supplies needed for arts and crafts, nature, Camp Craft and music and dance classes in the '60s. Magic markers were not widely used, nor were they inexpensive. Instead, we're talking paint, paintbrushes, paper, glue, staplers, scissors, tape, crayons, kits, boondoggle, clips, clay, pins, hand-held compasses, magnifying glasses, small musical instruments, records and a record player, handsaws, hatchets—again, the list goes on and on.

Careful planning and good maintenance kept Camp Onanda safe and well supplied in all areas.

Behind the scenes, nearly unnoticed by campers and counselors when camp was in full swing, were the folks making things flow. For most of the '60s, Skip (Barbara Fisher) was the camp director and D.J. (Dana Knisley) the program director. They kept a close eye on staff and campers, and that means they knew exactly where everyone was. They were quick to see a need and could make that need disappear just as quickly. They helped counselors develop teaching skills. They made sure that every aspect of every item at camp made for a safe experience. They knew the campers, encouraged the staff and met every special need. They simply kept all activities, attitudes and behaviors monitored and somehow resolved any problem that arose. They were amazing.

Dixie (Dorothy Dougan Widmer) was the business part of camp. Yes, there was a lot of business that needed tending to. Mail was sorted and delivered daily. Food was ordered for the entire camp. The camp store had to be stocked and run. If a cabin decided to take an overnight away from camp, that cabin needed food. The cabin would submit a requisition sheet of its campers' needs and wants, and Dixie would see to it that all items were there. Many counselors learned a lot from Dixie. As she filled a requisition, she easily noticed any obvious omission. It might be forks, a can opener or just something that would be nice to have but not entirely necessary. If a cabin's campers forgot this item on their requisition, they didn't get it. Once away from camp, campers and counselors survived, but they likely couldn't get back to camp for the wanted item that was not on the requisition. Items were not forgotten on future requisition forms. Lesson learned.

When a cabin was on an overnight away from camp, Skip and D.J. would check up on it, especially if that time away was a canoe trip. They would hop in the motorboat and make sure that the group had arrived at its destination safely. Sometimes they would even bring the forgotten item from the requisition if Dixie felt it was truly needed. Remember, there were no cellphones or easy means of communicating needs once away from camp.

Counselors were allowed free time after taps, though two Lower Camp and two Teen Hill counselors were assigned guard duty each night. If on guard duty, the counselors would walk their part of the camp, making sure campers were quiet and stayed put. Then, too, the night guard was there if a camper got sick or someone came onto camp grounds who shouldn't be there. The counselors with free time could go into town or simply lounge in Abode or plot a camp prank. Of course, the camp directors made sure all counselors were in their cabins by the midnight curfew. Skip and D.J. somehow knew exactly where their staff were at all times. It was, according to counselors, totally eerie how they would know when to be stationed at the camp gate. Somehow, they just knew when the gals would be returning from town.

Skip and D.J. were well aware of the comings and goings of their staff because they had three very effective things in place. First, they set up a system with the "hot spots" in town. If a gang of counselors went to the pizza place or anywhere in town, when they left the establishment, the owner would call camp and let them know the girls were returning. Second, they had Brandy, a buff cocker spaniel who let them know if anything "unusual" was unfolding on camp at night. Third, they had ears. Little House, their cabin, was situated very near Abode, the counselors' meeting and relaxing cabin. When counselors were plotting a prank or planning a night out while in Abode, Skip and D.J. often heard the discussion. The counselors were totally unaware of how their voices traveled.

Camp directors' duties were twenty-four-hour ones. It is a hard and endless job. End of report. Do you still want the job?

Just as common in the '60s as it is today, some campers needed daily medication. The camp nurse was on top of that. If a camper didn't show up at the prescribed time, she was found. No one missed needed medication. No scrape went unattended. While no major accident befell anyone at Onanda in the '60s, Band-Aids were administered and a stomach or two may have needed some time out. Records show that there was never a broken bone or the need for stitches in this decade. The biggest emergency was in the summer of '61 when a program director, while on a trip with campers to the Adirondack Mountains, had an appendicitis attack. Everyone survived. It might be interesting to note that not one camper was sent home for any sickness, including homesickness.

To assist in the flow were college-aged gals who were not assigned to a cabin but rather to an area or smaller group of staff. The waterfront director was on the waterfront everyday, keeping all aspects of the waterfront activities and equipment in order. A junior counselor director (April MacDonald for several summers of the '60s) kept tabs on the youngest counselors and helped them to be creative and responsible teachers and counselors. For the same reasons, a CIT director (Margaret "Perk" Wheeler held this position) planned all activities for this camper/staff transitional group. CITs were together in a cabin without a "resident" counselor.

Then, when something broke, a drain got blocked, a playing field needed mowing or something mechanical was not functioning correctly, Mr. Smeenk came to the rescue. Arnold Smeenk, with his family, lived in one of the homes on the camp property year-round for well over a decade. He was rightfully dubbed the "Keeper of Onanda," and keep Onanda safe and beautiful he did.

During the nine active and busy weeks of summer, he quietly kept all mechanical and landscape needs cared for. As soon as the camping season ended, he prepared all the buildings for winter and made any repairs he could. Come spring, he started to get things ready to be opened and safe for a new season. It was a job requiring all sorts of skills, and Arnold did it all with great respect and ability. Throughout most of the '60s and well into the

'70s, the Smeenk family made a huge impact on Onanda and were always a vital and loved part of the Onanda family.

Yes, behind the scenes were incredible leaders. This leadership is what provided a safe yet exciting summer adventure for thousands of girls.

While this was very much how Camp Onanda flowed during the eleven seasons Skip was at the helm, no matter what decade a girl attended Onanda, it was 99 percent likely that she never forgot her experience.

As the '60s came to a close, YWCA Camp Onanda turned fifty.

ONANDA MEETS THE '70s

The '70s began with the break up of the Beatles, Elvis Presley's death and Sony introducing the Walkman. Computer floppy disks, VCRs and pocket calculators were introduced. The first Earth Day was celebrated, the voting age was lowered from twenty-one to eighteen, and Microsoft was founded. The Vietnam War brought protests to college campuses, and the Watergate break-in forced President Nixon from office. Cigarettes could no longer be advertised on television, *Roe v. Wade* allowed women to abort a pregnancy. The Viking 1 Space probe landed on Mars, and American Pioneer 11 was the first spacecraft to pass Saturn. *M*A*S*H* premiered on TV, and the first *Star Wars* movie hit the big screen. The United States pulled out of Vietnam, the first test-tube baby was born and Iranian revolutionaries took American hostages in Tehran. While this was the decade of Apollo 13, Charles Manson, protests, government upheaval and setbacks of all kinds, the bicentennial of the United States was celebrated and helped us remember that our nation had survived much and made positive forward movement.

The year 1970 marked the sixty-fourth summer that the YWCA of Rochester had been involved on Canandaigua Lake and the fifty-first summer of activities at Camp Onanda since the YWCA had purchased the Foster land. No major changes had been made to Onanda since 1955.

As the summer of 1970 began, Hill House, now primarily used as the camp office, infirmary and residence for some of the staff, was showing its age. One of the original buildings on the property (the home of the Foster family when purchased by the Rochester YWCA), it had served Onanda well and needed major repairs. Back in the 1920s and until 1955, all meals were prepared and served in Hill House. During the 1950s modernization of Onanda, both the north and south porches of Hill House were remodeled to

Foster Home/Hill House. *Courtesy of the Albert R. Stone Collection, RMSC.*

provide two cabins for junior campers. This camp landmark had been used continually and hard for over one hundred years. To make this wonderful old home up-to-date and functional would be very costly. Sadly, it became obvious that it would be far more cost effective to tear down Hill House. Plans began to build a single-story building in its place. This new building would house the office and infirmary and add a nature room area. It was a hard decision to replace this historic home, but it was beyond restoration.

The dining hall, once a long section of Babcock Hall and now fifty years old, needed updating in order to efficiently provide the nearly thirty-six thousand meals during the summer camp season. This two-story building had never been fully insulated, though the kitchen area had been carefully installed to meet all safety regulations of 1955. Now ovens, stoves, refrigerators and even the dishwasher would have to be replaced. Because the second floor of the dinning hall acted as a dorm for some summer employees and housed visitors when the camp was rented during the off-season, it was decided that the dining hall should be entirely winterized.

Another major fundraising effort began at the Rochester YWCA. The costs were high, and raising the funds would be challenging.

As in the past, many folks invested a lot of time and energy to see this plan fall into place. Again, some supportive men rallied to the cause along with the many chapters of the YWCA. Edmund King was one man who had a soft spot in his heart for Camp Onanda.

In 1944, King was elected to the board of trustees of the YWCA of Rochester and Monroe County and was still ready to help Onanda in the '70s. He served as chairman of that board from 1963 to 1965 and was the board's first honorary member until his passing. Camp Onanda was King's baby in that he wanted to keep this camp in the spotlight as a successful and desired summer destination for girls. King was entirely involved with the major rebuilding of the camp in 1955. King Hall on Teen Hill was named in his honor in 1963. He also engineered the water system at camp, along with so many other projects that it was only natural that he assist with this newest improvement effort.

Another remarkable man, Jack Gorham, stepped up to the plate and hit a home run when this 1970 building plan started to bog down. Gorham had been highly involved with the YMCA getting a summer camp program started for boys in the early '60s. He had purchased land for the boys' camp in the Adirondack Mountains and set up an endowment for the YMCA camp that would be named in his honor. Camp Gorham is still operating just north of Eagle Bay, New York. Less than ten years after getting the boys' camp started, he learned that the YWCA was struggling to get funds for the renovations at Onanda. Knowing well the incredible value of outdoor education and recreation, Gorham provided $75,000 and his time to see Camp Onanda through a tough fundraiser. Gorham's rescue did not go unnoticed. The new and improved dining hall at Camp Onanda, Gorham Hall, still carries his name.

On June 1, 1972, with all improvements made, Camp Onanda was again in full swing, ready and waiting for the girls of summer and all groups that would spend time there.

As this decade began, Kammy and Hilary were returning for their eighth summer at camp, starting their second summer as junior counselors. Having enjoyed so many summers as campers, they now "paid it back" by helping to make memories for new campers and new memories for themselves as staff. Once in camp, reunited with old friends and making introductions with the new staff, Kammy made her personal and traditional pre-camp hike up the Teen Hill road. As she started this solo hike up the rugged, tree-shrouded dirt road, she reflected on summers past and the adventures that surely would lie ahead. Just as the muscles in her legs remembered the steepness of this hike, Kammy reached Kiniks, the first cabin perched on Teen Hill. She walked a

Teen Hill. *Author's collection.*

few yards farther into the open and well-groomed cabin hillside and finally looked to her right. Yes, she was back! That glorious lake view, the pine and woods smells and birds chattering their welcome brought that peace and calm to her that called her back to Onanda summer after summer.

Pre-Camp, the week of staff orientation, flowed as usual with Skip and D.J. at the helm. This was a time of meetings and preparation but also one of bonding. Even though a busy time, it never failed in pulling together a diverse and multi-aged staff into one eager, talented and unified group. Their goal: provide an unforgettable summer experience for girls.

The waterfront staff, as required from the start, was all Red Cross certified. They held certifications as lifeguards and water safety instructors and in boating and first aid—you name the Red Cross certification, and someone on the staff had it. Nature, arts and crafts, Camp Crafts, tennis, music and dance, folk art, creative writing, archery and riflery staff all had experience and knowledge in the area they taught. It is no wonder that classes were fun, safe and educational.

The summer of 1970 was Sarah Gleason's second summer at Camp Onanda as a camper. She had come the summer before with her friend Julie, and though they did not end up in the same cabin, they had had a blast and were ready for another summer at Onanda. Her first summer was experienced in Wikis in Lower Camp, but this summer, she was moving on up to Teen Hill. This summer she would be in Tona. Like it would for so many others, Camp Onanda would call Sarah back for many years.

The 1970s were most definitely years of great social change. The YWCA of Rochester was now facing those changes by taking a stand for abortion rights, civil rights, getting involved with the Attica Defense

Fund and working toward beginning a new program called RESTART (a comprehensive program to deal with heroin addicts) while trying to fund its Campership Program for Onanda. The Campership Program was a scholarship program allowing girls from low-income families to attend camp. The 1974 records show that $1,184 was available for scholarships, but the requests for camperships far outnumbered the ability to grant them.

While these social changes put new pressures on the YWCA's goal to be ever outreaching, changes in leadership came to Camp Onanda. For over a decade, Onanda had prospered and grown under the same leadership, with many of the same staff returning summer after summer. This consistency in leadership and staff made for a really good flow at Onanda. With the torch passed to a new camp director, and the YWCA getting deeply involved with new programs beyond the camp, Onanda struggled some to keep the attention and support of the Rochester YWCA on its programs.

Even so, traditions at camp pretty much stayed in tact, with camper shows, staff shows, wish boat ceremonies, nightly campfires and singing. Campers were still finding friendships and making those memories that would last their lifetimes.

Waterfront classes stayed pretty much the same, but a new class or two would be added as the skills and interests of the staff changed. Some summers synchronized swimming and diving were offered because someone on the staff was able to share those skills, and others summers they were not. The staples were all levels of swimming, boating, canoeing, water skiing and sailing.

Riflery was an offering that only Teen Hill girls were involved with. Obviously, there were many safety reasons for this to be offered to elder girls only, as a slew of rules and regulations had to be met. Cap was the counselor involved right from its introduction as a class offering in the '60s. She had to keep up with all requirements to teach it and keep Onanda's range and guns up to regulation. The demanded regulations were met, but attitudes toward guns had changed. In the '70s, riflery was eliminated from Onanda's list of classes.

It was a gal named Agnes that truly disrupted the start of camp in 1972. Agnes started the trek to New York from the Gulf of Mexico around June 14, arriving in New York around June 23 and bringing an incredible amount of water. Agnes started out as a Category 1 hurricane, and by the time it reached Pennsylvania and New York, the collected water had created incredible devastation. The upper Genesee River, south of the Mount Morris Dam, was flooded to a historical high. Roads and bridges were washed out, and the debris and water flowing north caused all sorts of damage. At the time, Agnes was the costliest hurricane to hit the United States.

Agnes pulled into Camp Onanda on Friday, June 23, with terrific wind and pelting rain. Arnold, the on-site caretaker, saw that the canoes and row boats had to be moved as Canandaigua's water kept creeping into camp. He and his son Kevin headed into the storm and moved the twenty-some boats away from the rising water, but by the time they had accomplished this, it was apparent that they hadn't moved them far enough. It was equally apparent that the docks would not survive the battering waves, so those too were pulled in. The lake was wild; six-foot waves and the torrential rain were simply taking over the waterfront. They moved the boats farther and then pulled the docks farther. Agnes just kept coming, so the dock sections and boats had to keep moving too.

By Saturday, there was no change. Huge waves pounded into camp, rain continued and the Lower Camp campfire circle was now a part of the lake. Then, a really huge problem was discovered. The pump house, the source of pumped water for the entire camp, was in danger. If the pumps got submerged by this onslaught of water, they would be worthless. If they were disconnected, there would be no source of water for the entire camp!

Arnold came up with a plan. With help from Skip, Kevin and Hawkes, they got the pumps up higher by putting them on cement blocks. With waves crashing and rain and wind constant, he also felt the pumps should be disconnected as a precaution. This was done in howling wind and rising water, and they noticed that the boats would need to be moved yet again.

Though the boathouse was being slammed by waves, the Lower Camp cabins were elevated high enough and far enough from the original and now flooded shoreline that water wasn't yet getting inside them. Still, a watchful eye had to be kept on a couple cabins that were nearest the waterfront.

Having done all that four people could do to protect, preserve and defend the pumps, buildings and boats, Skip now had to inform the summer staff that Pre-Camp would not start the next day. There was no way to cook for sixty people without running water, and of course, the washhouses could not be used with the pumps disconnected. The camp was inundated. Agnes was still delivering wind and rain. No, starting Pre-Camp was not an option. Now calls had to go out to tell the staff to stay home.

The summer staff lived all over, some out of state, some closer. Near or far away, word reached the staff that Pre-Camp was postponed. This was the first time *ever* that Pre-Camp had been delayed.

As the water, ever so slowly, began to calm, the pumps were reconnected, and Pre-Camp started on the following Wednesday. Of course, Lower Camp had a whole new look as the staff arrived. The waterfront was now about thirty feet closer to cabins, and the campfire circle was still in water. Though they had lost three days of training, the staff pulled together quickly. They cleaned up areas and reorganized the boats and dock that were nearly up to the new office/nature building.

There would be no swimming until the third session that summer, when the water was safe to swim in and the beach and water free from debris, so new classes were implemented for the first two sessions. Swimming was a huge loss for a waterfront camp, but Skip said the staff were incredibly creative and came up with all sorts of things to do instead of swimming and water skiing. More classes were offered in boating, canoeing and sailing, and for the first time in years, fishing became a popular activity again.

The loss of the Lower Camp campfire circle was huge. Nightly campfires were such a major part of the Onanda experience. Campfires were like Elmer's Glue in that they bonded campers and staff. Yet even a storm the likes of Agnes didn't take away one campfire. As the land started to dry and return to normal, Lower Camp had its evening campfire in Crouch Hall. Teen Hill had no water issues, so every night, the air surrounding Camp Onanda was filled with the usual laughter and music that had been heard every summer's night since 1909.

Though Agnes created a huge amount of unexpected extra preparation, Camp Onanda still did what she always did—provided a rare and wonderful summer experience for campers. The loss of waterfront classes for the first four weeks of 1972 would not diminish Onanda. Memories were secured.

An entirely different challenge started the summer of '73. After a decade plus under the leadership of Skip, a steady period of leadership change began. Alice Hamlin saw Onanda through the summer of '73 as an interim director. Then, the following three summers, Pat Collins took on the leadership. Marion Herz came in 1977 and Lydia Pettis put her mark on Onanda as camp director from 1978 through 1980. With the focus of the Rochester YWCA changing, the camp directors were challenged to keep Onanda on Rochester Y's agenda, but keep it there they did as well as they could.

Meanwhile, with five changes in camp directors in the decade of the '70s, changes in the staff and campers came, too. The seasoned and cherished caretaker Arnold retired in the summer of '75. Counselors didn't seem to be returning summer after summer, as they had done in the

Agnes floods Onanda. *Courtesy of the Fisher/Knisley Collection.*

past. Summer sessions didn't always have a waiting list, but campers came and still enjoyed the adventures that only summer camp provided. The camp directors and counselors were still firmly dedicated to helping make those lifelong memories.

Still, the signs of change and focus at the downtown YWCA, though not entirely apparent to campers and counselors of Camp Onanda, were slowly creeping into the flow of camp. By the end of the decade, likely unknown to those involved at Onanda, Onanda's future would become questionable.

In the first eight years of this decade, Sarah Gleason was at Onanda as a camper, then as a CIT, a junior counselor and finally as a counselor. She was the rare exception now, being a part of Onanda so continually, but Sarah forged ahead, offering her experience to make new adventures for new campers.

As a camper, she enjoyed her classes on the waterfront and arts and crafts the best. Since she never acquired the necessary Red Cross certifications, as a counselor she taught archery, nature and creative writing. Ever looking to provide new experiences for campers, as a junior counselor, Sarah developed a new class that she called Folk Arts. She set up an area where her charges did activities such as dipping candles; churning butter; carding, dyeing and spinning wool; and making ice cream. She claimed it fit her earthy, hippie side to a T.

Sarah was by no means alone in keeping creative, memorable and absolutely fun activities flowing at Onanda. Camp classes and activities adapted with the changes in staff, but traditions held strong.

No matter from what decade a girl attended camp, memories of time spent at Onanda had common threads. From the 1920s to the '80s, camp was about laughter, friendships and personal growth.

Often campers and counselors said that when they came to camp the first time, they were shy or had emotional issues that come with youth. There were simply things in their lives that made them more withdrawn or cautious or just sense that they were not readily accepted. Camp Onanda changed all that. At camp, girls felt they were a part of the adventure and not so different from others. At camp, there were no pressures from or expectations made by family. A girl could try new skills without being graded by a teacher. Of course, there were rules and schedules to be kept, but within those confines, there were new opportunities and choices to make each day. Having the chance to try things without worry of failure because you could try again and having choices that could be made without pressure from others was empowering and life changing. Sure, some choices didn't turn out as anticipated but presented a personal learning experience. Choices would become thoughtful and not so dependent on others. Choices would be one of the best parts of camp and learning to choose would be lesson carried throughout life.

Cat "Mouser" Holmes expressed the change Onanda made for her so colorfully. Before going to Onanda, she shared, her vision was in black and white. Onanda changed it to Technicolor.

4

Camp Onanda Passes Her Torch

THE FINAL YEARS OF CAMP ONANDA AND BIRTH OF ONANDA PARK

The 1980s started out with bang—Mount St. Helens erupted! The Pac-Man video game was released; Rubik's Cubes, Cabbage Patch Kids and the movie *E.T.* entertained Americans. Assassination attempts were made on the Pope and President Reagan. Indira Gandhi and John Lennon were killed. Sally Ride became the first woman in space, and the space shuttle *Challenger* exploded on takeoff, killing the seven astronauts, Christa McAuliffe, the first civilian teacher, among them. IBM introduced personal computers, a hole in the Ozone layer was discovered and the wreck of the *Titanic* was found. This decade introduced the first disc cameras, compact discs, mobile phones, camcorders, Macintosh PCs, disposable contact lenses and Nintendo's Game Boy (a handheld video game player). The Berlin Wall came down, ending the cold war and reuniting Germany. MTV, TNT and CNN were born, as was Prince Charles and Lady Diana's first child, Prince William. Queen, Kools & the Gang, AC/DC, the Rolling Stones, Michael Jackson, Lionel Richie, Culture Club, Stevie Wonder, REO Speedwagon, Madonna, Bon Jovi, Guns N' Roses, Whitney Houston, Metallica and others sang their way through this decade. The first Persian Gulf War, the discovery of AIDS, war between Great Britain and Argentina, bombing of the U.S. embassy in Beirut, the Iran-Contra Affair, Black Monday (global stock market crash) and the Tiananmen Square Massacre in China all kept the world a little on edge. This decade ended with the initial proposal for the World Wide Web that would eventually be accessible to everyone as a source of information.

As the World Changes So Changes Camp Onanda

The decade of the '80s started out fairly routinely for Camp Onanda in that the summer programs began as usual. Counselors arrived for Pre-Camp orientation, and campers filled the summer air with laughter and songs. The girls of summer didn't always fill each session, but those who did come enjoyed all that made this camp a special place.

In 1982, Onanda would be shared with a new and special group of young people.

In 1979, Gary Mervis and his wife had a nightmare unfold in their lives. Their nine-year-old daughter, Teddi, began a rough struggle with cancer. As she bravely battled through the medical attempts to save her life, Teddi felt entirely isolated from her peers. Back then, cancer was not something

The Camp Good Days logo. *Author's collection.*

people talked about. It was a horror that families faced pretty much alone. The Mervises agonized over Teddi's loneliness and had nothing to offer her in terms of connecting her with other kids with this life-threatening disease. While they could and did find her all the medical support of the time, there were no support groups for kids or families dealing with cancer. Though their hearts ached, the Mervises created a rare and wonderful but normal and fun camping experience for their daughter and thousands of other children faced with life-threatening illnesses.

Mr. and Mrs. Mervis came up with an idea, and with the help of some dear friends, Camp Good Days and Special Times was born. This camp would be for sick kids. Originally, this camp would bring together for five days of outdoor fun kids who were faced with the isolation that came with having cancer. This camp would provide a normal situation where sick kids could share their battle with cancer while simply doing what regular kids enjoyed doing—playing, singing and making friends at summer camp. There would be no cost involved for campers.

Just finding a place to safely accommodate kids with such extreme needs wasn't easy. In 1979, established camps were pretty much in use during the summer months and lesser-used camps were simply not accessible or in such disrepair that they wouldn't work. As word started getting out about the hope of starting a camp for kids with cancer, more people started stepping up to help. Joseph "Bello" Snyder, the owner of Camp Eagle Cove on Fourth Lake in the Adirondack Mountains, remembered Mr. Mervis from high school sports and offered his camp at no charge when it wasn't involved with its regular summer camping and basketball camps. The first three gatherings of Camp Good Days and Special Times were spent on Fourth Lake, and Teddi lived long enough to experience the first two years.

The greatest problem with this location was the distance from the sort of medical help these special campers might need. Though arrangements were made with state police for speedy assistance if needed, a search was ever active to find a location within a sixty-mile radius of the University of Rochester medical complex.

By the summer of 1982, Camp Good Days and Special Times would begin to have a presence at Camp Onanda. The location allowed for children from Buffalo, Syracuse and Albany medical centers to join those from the University of Rochester. With a volunteer staff, including doctors, and the closer medical center, more kids could be safely involved with this rare experience.

The Ninety-eighth Division Army Reserve stepped up to help Camp Good Days. *Courtesy of Gary Mervis.*

The updates made to Camp Onanda in the '70s provided for fairly reasonable access, and closer proximity to medical help put parents of campers more at ease. A major problem Camp Good Days and Special Times faced as it considered Onanda for its location was finding a cooking staff that would volunteer their time and skill for a large and hungry group of campers.

Enter the Ninety-eighth Division Army Reserve. No kidding, the army reservists came to serve and quickly became entirely involved and connected with the campers of Camp Good Days. They didn't just serve up great meals; they were also an integral part of the campers' experience.

Then, too, the support from law enforcement was beyond the call. When any issue arose, no matter how severe or seemingly minor, the Ontario County Sheriffs were ready to assist. When Steve, a camper, faced a stressful situation, in came the Ontario County Sheriffs.

Steve came to Camp Onanda/Camp Good Days with a very, very special stuffed animal. This animal had been with Steve from his first chemo treatment and could not be left at home. Shortly after Steve arrived, something worse than cancer happened. He couldn't find his stuffed buddy.

Inconsolable, Steve started his walk home. He couldn't face camp without his stuffed buddy, so he was going home. Mr. Mervis caught up with Steve and asked what the problem was. This was, indeed, a very bad thing, but Mr. Mervis knew exactly what to do. He told Steve that they needed to get the police involved to help find his buddy.

Within minutes of calling the sheriff's office, the police were on the scene. They came by boat, car and motorcycle. A report was made as Steve described his buddy and where he had last seen his stuffed animal. While this was all taken very seriously, there was a dreaded concern among the adults that the missing animal would not be found.

To do their part as a camp, all the campers lined up arm in arm and began their search of Camp Onanda for Steve's lost pal. These campers knew too well how important this stuffed animal was. They slowly and carefully crossed the camp and—yes, it was found!

While this was the happiest of endings, it wasn't really the end. A day later, the Ontario County Sheriffs returned to camp and made Steve an honorary deputy sheriff. From that day onward, Steve was known as Sheriff Steve. Now there's an incredible ending that surely carried Sheriff Steve through all his days.

For seven years, Camp Onanda welcomed the campers of Camp Good Days and Special Times. They enjoyed the waterfront and had classes in arts and crafts, music and all the sorts of things you'd expect at summer camp.

Sheriff Steve and pals. *Courtesy of Gary Mervis.*

The staff and Good Days campers at Onanda. *Courtesy of Gary Mervis.*

Mr. Mervis, a humble and gentle man, will tell you that Camp Good Days and Special Times may have been his dream of giving kids with cancer a place to be regular kids and a forever tribute to his daughter Teddi, but he quickly adds that it never would have developed into the organization it is today without the constant and fabulous support of many.

If you would like to know more about Camp Good Days, you'll find a wonderful site at www.campgooddays.org. You can truly get to know Teddi Mervis by reading *For the Love of Teddi—The Story Behind Camp Good Days and Special Times* by Lou Buttino.

Today, the Camp Good Days organization reaches out to all people dealing with cancer, adding support and gatherings for adults as well. It

continues to expand its work with children who face not only cancer and all sorts of life-threatening diseases but also violent situations. Camp Onanda was blessed to be a small part of the history of this incredible organization.

Meanwhile, back at the Rochester YWCA, urban concerns grew. The services and programs provided for the city were vital and costly. Finances for these programs and services were dwindling quickly, and decisions had to be made.

As this decade began, Camp Onanda was yet a bright spot in the YWCA's mind, but it wasn't always drawing in the number of campers it had in the past. The costs of insurance, maintaining the property year-round and operating it in the summer just seemed to be more and more overwhelming. With its focus strongly on the needs of Rochester's youth and struggling women in Rochester, the YWCA began the difficult process of sorting through the feasibility of keeping Camp Onanda. It was a soul-searching period, but the final decision was to sell the camp.

Regular summer sessions would unfold at Onanda through the onset of the decade, but little did campers and counselors of the summer of 1987 realize that that year would be the last summer of YWCA-sponsored camping at Onanda.

As the summer of 1988 neared, even though campers had signed on for a session of fun at Camp Onanda, the YWCA suddenly announced that camp would not be held. The decision had been made. Onanda would be sold, and this left parents scrambling to get their daughters placed at other camps. While it was a truly sad way to end the rich and wonderful history of summer camp, the YWCA saw no other option.

Once word of this sudden closing reached the ear of Mr. M. James Holden, the town of Canandaigua supervisor, he knew the value of this land. If for sale, the access to the lake would be an immense acquisition for the town. There were few public access areas around the lake, and all other lakefront land was privately owned. Never would an opportunity to have a large piece of land and 160 feet of lakefront land arise again. Camp Onanda would provide that and so much more for the lake community and visitors to the area. Yes, the Town of Canandaigua was very, very interested in acquiring this land for public use and went into action.

Instantly upon learning of the possible sale of Camp Onanda, the Town of Canandaigua hired an assessor to determine the potential value of this land. By February 15, 1989, Eastern Appraisal Associates, LTD, presented an eighty-page appraisal of the land that had been Camp Onanda for Holden. The author of the assessment was extremely thorough. On page fifty-nine he wrote, "A common thread running through this appraisal report is that the subject property is at once a unique property, and one of the most attractive and desirable parcels in its general neighborhood. It is, however, an enigma." That "enigma," for him, was all the buildings that didn't add value to the land. When all of Onanda was viewed by eye, photographed from the air, surveyed and assessed, the value of the property was set at $2.2 million.

Meanwhile, back in Albany, New York, the Department of Environment and Conservation (DEC) of the state of New York realized the value in the lakefront land as well. The DEC saw a need for access to the lake. It had no official area to monitor the lake's health and the safety of boaters and fishers. The State of New York could make this area a state park. Instead, it struck a plan with the Town of Canandaigua. If a "deal" could be made, the state would pay $2 million and own the smaller acreage of the lakefront land, and the town would pay the remaining amount and own the larger upland

The Town of Canandaigua purchases Onanda. *From the* Daily Messenger.

acreage. The state further agreed that the development and maintenance of the entire purchase would be given to the Town of Canandaigua. It would simply not interfere with any of the plans the town saw fit to implement at Onanda Park.

News broke in the Rochester and Canandaigua newspapers on April 18, 1989, that the YWCA of Rochester and Monroe County and the Town of Canandaigua had signed an agreement.

Then the challenges began. Apparently, some of Onanda's neighbors were not at all happy with the idea that the former camp would become a public park. They wanted information. They wanted to know the details of this purchase, the terms of the agreement with the state and how this purchase would affect their lives. They definitely voiced a fear that a public park next to their private homes and cottages would lower the value of their land. They felt this deal had been made in secrecy, and they wanted to be heard.

At first glance, it seems a tad odd that these same neighbors bought their private land knowing full well that a girls' summer camp was next to them but now were highly distressed that it would become a public park. A closer look at this situation justified some of their unrest. As a privately owned camp, Onanda did not have cars and people coming and going all day. Nights were quiet, and frankly, the entire camp was so highly regulated that most of

Onanda's neighbors hardly noticed the goings on next door. Opening this area to the public was an entirely different ball of wax.

Knowing that car traffic would increase, they questioned where folks would park those cars. If overnight stays were allowed, their concerns grew. Would overnight campers be allowed to arrive with their own trailers and tents and would arrival and departure times be regulated? What about restrictions on alcohol consumption and large groups using the park? How would boundaries be set so visitors didn't wander onto private cottage and home areas? How would rules and restrictions be enforced? Simply put, the neighbors of Camp Onanda saw a plethora of issues that would affect their families. These issues needed addressing, and initially, they were feeling left out of the process.

In July 1989, just two months from the proposed transfer of Camp Onanda to Onanda Park, this battle hit the local papers. The purchase would not be a done deal until the lawsuit was settled.

The town made some major and definite concessions to the use of and rules for the public park, but it would not let go of the right for overnight camping. As it turned out, this issue of allowing overnight camping was the major focus of the dispute.

The lawsuit dropped into the lap of state Supreme Court justice Wilmer J. Patlow. Justice Patlow strongly urged both parties to reach an out-of-court settlement. While this battle was still going on, the town took official ownership of Camp Onanda from the YWCA on August 7, 1989. This, of course, infuriated those issuing the lawsuit all the more, but an agreement was indeed reached.

Parking issues would be settled and overnight camping would be established but not in tents or campers. Overnight camping would become

There were snags in the plan. *From the* Rochester Democrat and Chronicle.

available only by renting cabins that were already on the property. Also, no alcohol would be allowed in the park, ever.

Finally, the Town of Canandaigua was able and ready to pursue its hopes and dreams for Onanda Park.

FINAL FAREWELLS TO CAMP ONANDA

Though the camp was now the property of the Town of Canandaigua and the DEC, an invitation went out from the Rochester YWCA to say farewell to Camp Onanda.

The day, Saturday, August 19, 1989, arrived with sunshine but with no exceptional warmth in the air or in the hearts of former campers and staff of Camp Onanda. This reunion was sad. Former campers, counselors and staff came to witness the official turning over of their beloved camp to the Town of Canandaigua and the DEC. Officials from the Rochester

YWCA had set up tables with old photographs and memorabilia documenting the nearly eighty years of history Onanda had had on Canandaigua Lake. T-shirts commemorating the day were for sale. Lower Camp buildings were open for final visits.

It was a day of mini-reunions for girls and women from various summers spent at camp, but those reunions were dampened with the knowledge that no other young girls would have

YWCA CAMP ONANDA'S GREAT REUNION

Saturday, Aug. 19
11 a.m. to 4:30 p.m.
at Camp Onanda on Canandaigua Lake
(Rain date: Aug. 20)

Join us to reminisce and say farewell to Camp Onanda

Swimming
Glen sliding
Picnicking
(food available or bring your own)
Souvenirs
Nostalgic photo displays
Prizes

For former Camp Onanda campers, staff, volunteers and other friends of the YWCA

Souvenirs will be given to the first 250 people to attend.
T-shirts available for sale. Brief program at 2 p.m.

Attendance is free but please call YWCA membership services at 546-5820 to let us know you're coming.

SPREAD THE WORD!

A United Way Agency   YWCA Rochester & Monroe County

A sad reunion. *Author's collection.*

similar reunions. Still, final hikes were taken up Teen Hill to cabins that held fond memories. Stories of cabin adventures were told again as though they had taken place the past summer when it had been nearly twenty summers prior. Walks up the glen were a must. From the waterfront to the far reaches of the camp, small knots of women and girls paused to share remembered antics and friendships.

Around two o'clock in the afternoon, folks gathered in Lowe Chapel, the outdoor area set aside for Sunday services when Camp Onanda was thriving. The history of the camp was shared, as were memories and one letter in particular that had been sent to the YWCA by a former counselor.

19 August 1989

Dear Onanda,

It is no wonder that you remain a vivid, vital part of my spirit. You have touched the souls of the Senecas who called your water The Chosen Spot, Canandaigua. Hundreds of moons later, you let me know your history, feel your sparkling water, see your sun rise, and hear your joy of life and laughter. Onanda, every moc, every sneaker, every bare foot that has paced your shore, traveled your glen or hiked your hill has been touched by your gifts.

You have been through many changes since the Senecas grew from you. White men from New England and Virginia found your beauty. Mr. Phelps and Mr. Gorham sensed your kindness and kept your name. They brought rugged individuals to The Chosen Spot who civilized the land without taking too much from it in return. All those who have come somehow knew that this lake with rolling hills and shale cliffs should remain as close to nature as possible.

Today Canandaigua is dotted with summer homes, cottages and gentle communities. One can still imagine the Senecas coming to your shore for water, fishing from the lake and canoeing the waterway with furs to trade. Like the area, Onanda, you too must change. Fear not, though, for you will remain open. Open to souls that you will be able to touch with your past and imprint with your spirit. You will still hear laughter and feel the blaze of cooking fires. Though change is difficult and secrets you have held will vanish, you will always be a powerful influence upon those who feel you.

I will miss the cabins resting high on Onanda's hill. But then I will think of how the Senecas must have felt when their open land became obstructed by dwellings of white men. And, like the Senecas, I will never forget how it once was because one can't forget those things in life that touch the inner most part of one's spirit.

All that I ask, all that I hope for is that Onanda will be allowed to ever share the wonder and secrets of her past and beauty. Onanda will continue to give if we tread lightly and open our hearts and minds to all that have made Onanda a slice of The Chosen Spot.

With tears and laughter of memories I must say good-bye to you, Onanda. The good-bye is to a landscape that taught me about friendship, giving and growth. No one will see you or know you as I did. Thank you for giving so freely of yourself.

May you always touch the spirits of those who meet you as you have mine. And may your visitors hear your wisdom and know your beauty. You are a gift, a Chosen Place, to those who will receive you. Hold fast dear friend.

This reunion was somber for the most part, but some joy would come from the fact that Camp Onanda would now become a place to be shared by the public. Camp Onanda would now be known as Onanda Park, cared for by the Town of Canandaigua.

Yes, change had come, but there would be no forgetting the friendships, laughter and songs of YWCA Camp Onanda.

So it was, on that August day of 1989, that the YWCA of Rochester said its final farewell to Camp Onanda. While it was a bittersweet transaction—bitter in that it was no longer a summer camp for girls, sweet because the land would retain it's name and be open to the public—the town had great plans for Onanda Park.

HELLO, ONANDA PARK!

With the purchase of Camp Onanda complete and disputes settled, the Town of Canandaigua wasted no time in making this land a public park. Onanda Park, as it would forever be known, was a huge endeavor that needed committed leadership. The town found that in Dennis Brewer.

By the fall of 1989, the town had put its sights on hiring Dennis to be the recreation director, but Dennis was not ready or eager to leave his teaching and coaching positions. Dennis shared his initial thoughts about joining the Onanda Park team.

In the fall of 1989, I received a phone call from Jane Alden, who was the part-time recreation director for the Town of Canandaigua. She oversaw the programs for the West Lake Schoolhouse/Beach and Leonard R. Pierce Park in Cheshire. The town had acquired the YWCA Camp and she wanted to know if I would be interested in taking her job as recreation director as she was leaving the position.

"Thanks for asking but no thanks," was my response. At the time, I was teaching sixth grade in Canandaigua as well as coaching freshmen basketball, girls' varsity soccer and middle school track and field. The next call was from Robert Simpson, the town supervisor, who felt I would be right for the position, but I declined. I continued to receive calls from town board members plus repeat calls from Robert and Jane. Finally I gave in and said I would be willing to take the position. I continued to teach and coach soccer but gave up basketball and track/field.

This reluctant leader would not only join the team but would also have a hand in all things Onanda Park.

Around 1994, Brewer would have the title of director of parks and recreation and would oversee all aspects of the town's parks. No longer a full-time teacher but always a substitute teacher if needed, he was now fully involved with developing Onanda Park and the town's other, smaller parks.

In this new position at Onanda, he planned which structures would be removed and which would be updated. He did all this with an aesthetic eye, keeping the park in harmony with nature. While many of the original cabins were removed, he oversaw the replacement of some buildings with wonderful pavilions and the construction of new cabins for renting. He also would develop rules and procedures for the park, hire guards and other summer staff while developing and often leading programs in fishing, canoeing and arts and crafts.

Jeff Winner, the caretaker of Camp Onanda, became part of the purchase of the camp. His knowledge of the property and its buildings was a bonus. He would continue to live year-round on the property and work closely with Brewer in transforming the camp into a public park.

The official opening of Onanda Park to the public came on July 1, 1990. At this time, the beach was open for swimming. Lifeguards were in place. Recreation classes were offered in arts and crafts, canoeing, fishing and Nature Nuts.

Prior to this grand opening, an order was placed for playground structures at a cost of $5,373. They would be placed near Crouch Hall. Needing a lifeguard station, a room for classes and an office, the inner walls of the camp office were taken down, and the building was reconfigured for park use. A fence between property's northern neighbor and the camp was replaced, the cost shared by the town and property owner. The old camp sign came down, and the new Onanda Park sign went up at the entrance. The sheriff's boathouse plans were discussed as well. Rates for classes and seasonal passes to the park were established. The Nature Nuts class would start on July 5 at $3 for residents and $6 for nonresidents. Seasonal passes would be $25 and $50, according to residency.

The first summer was one of discovering how to meet the needs of the park's neighbors as well as its visitors. When the park closed on Labor Day that first summer, plans and work began for the next summer season.

The spring of 1991 found Marty Dodge, an instructor at the Community College of the Finger Lakes, planning hiking trails for Onanda Park. He and fifteen of his students worked at clearing trails through the upland section (the land across West Lake Road) of the park. In the May 7, 1992 minutes of the recreation board, Dodge gave his update on their progress and his hope that the trail would be completed by July or August of that year.

Much work was needed to prepare for overnight stays. Some of the original cabins on the lakeside of the park were in great need of repair or were just not conducive for renting. Some were taken down. The washhouses needed to be updated to accommodate men and women. Decisions were made about the cabins on the hill too. Some would stay, but others would be taken down or moved to another location on the hillside. Crouch Hall would be remodeled, and new windows and doors would be added.

Onanda Park became an ideal place for groups to gather for a day of outdoor fun. But weather was always factor. Brewer and his staff knew well that a summer rain could suddenly roll over the western hills, and while they couldn't control that, they could and did build wonderful pavilions around the park. In Lower Camp, a huge pavilion near the waterfront was named for and dedicated to Mr. M. James Holden. His tireless effort to acquire the land would never be forgotten. Pavilions would be built on the hill and in Lower Camp so that no matter what weather came to Canandaigua Lake, Onanda Park was ready with shelter from the storm.

ONANDA PARK TODAY

Though always a work in progress, Onanda Park remains in the nurturing hands of Brewer and now offers cabins for overnight rental along with all sorts of daily programs for children. Hiking trails are well established and walks up the glen are still enjoyed. The waterfront is open for swimming when guards are on duty, and fishing is allowed farther down the shore. On any given day, picnics are enjoyed on what was Teen Hill or the waterfront. Not surprisingly, families are now bringing their children to Onanda Park yearly for that overnight experience of camping.

Onanda Park is as active today as it was when young girls ruled the summers. It remains a chosen spot that now welcomes everyone for a day on the lake or overnight accommodations. Go to www.townofcanandaigua.org to plan your visit.

All that remains to be done is for you to take a swim at Onanda Park, make that hike up the old road or new paths to the Upland Area of the park and make your history.

5

Onanda's Impact

YWCA Camp Onanda welcomed young, single women and then young girls to the shore of Canandaigua Lake for nearly eighty years. Onanda provided family camping, cheerleading camp, senior camping and church retreats, reaching out to all sorts of groups throughout the years. Any experience there enriched those who came, but the girls of summer camp have never forgotten their experiences or the impact it made on their lives.

A truly rough estimate—let's say from the mid-1920s, when young campers regularly started coming to Onanda, to the summer of 1985—would suggest that about 42,250 young girls spent at least a week at summer camp. While some gals said that camp wasn't exactly what they expected, almost everyone had a story of friendships made.

Dorothy Wright, born in 1912, still had a sparkle in her eyes at age ninety-nine when sharing about her Onanda experience in the early 1920s. She claimed that she didn't remember much but her fondest memory was of riding a horse. When Dorothy was at camp the land across the road was still the Dunn family farm. The Dunn's provided guided rides on their ponies and Dorothy never forgot the thrill of it.

Teeney Levi spent three summers at Onanda in the late 1930s. In her album, she wrote of friendships, arts and crafts projects and digging a pond on camp. Teeney just loved all the activities and freedom of spirit at camp.

Mentioned before, it was required, at least once each session, for campers to send a letter home. A simple postcard was acceptable, but some campers actually took the time to write letters. Important questions

Third session campers, 1966. *Courtesy of Nancy Showalter-Clark.*

Onanda staff, 1969. *Courtesy of Nancy Showalter-Clark.*

or "urgent" needs were often addressed since the camp experience was often the first time away from home for many of the younger girls.

Anne Morris (now Anne Mancilla), who was at Onanda in the '50s, remembers writing home to her mom with this urgent question: "Is it OK to wash my socks in shampoo?" Wouldn't you have loved to see Anne's mom's face as she read this?

Candy Campbell (now Candi Smith) was ten years old during the summer of 1958. It was her first summer at camp. Her mom, Helen, had sent her off to camp thinking that Candy would enjoy Onanda as much as her brother had enjoyed his Scout camp experience.

Well, Candy headed to camp not knowing anyone. Yes, she made lifelong friends in Maureen and Anne, but she found herself a tad frustrated and bored because she was not allowed in boats of any sort while at camp. The YWCA, ever aware of the dangers the lake presented, did not allow beginner

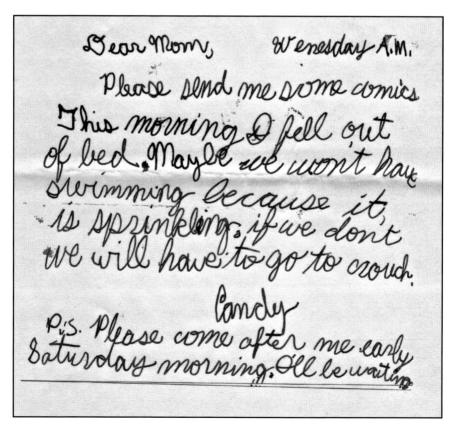

Dear Mom 1. *Courtesy of Candi Smith.*

Dear Mom 2. *Courtesy of Candi Smith.*

swimmers in boats of any shape or kind without a waterfront counselor on board. Very wise, but for Candy, this was very frustrating.

Candy wasn't the sort of girl to carry on with her disappointments, but she did vent some in her letters home. Bless her mom for saving those letters! As you read Candy's letters, put the voice of a ten-year-old of the late 1950s in your head.

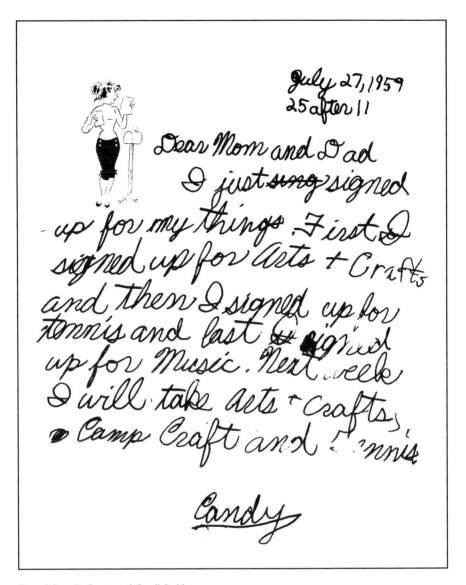

Dear Mom 3. *Courtesy of Candi Smith.*

Today, Candi doesn't recall that her mom sent the comic books or the deck of cards, but she did, indeed, send her daughter a care package that included candy. Yes, Candi smiles now and admits to trying to make her mom feel guilty about "abandoning her child at a summer camp." It worked somewhat, too, because she had a sleeping bag the next summer.

Candy's letters home the following summer didn't mention the dangers of wasps, falling out of bed or even questionable weather. Now an "experienced" camper, Candy shared what classes she had signed up for, the pancakes for breakfast, something special she had made and a costume ball that was to come. No, the second summer Mom and Dad Campbell didn't suffer any guilt trips.

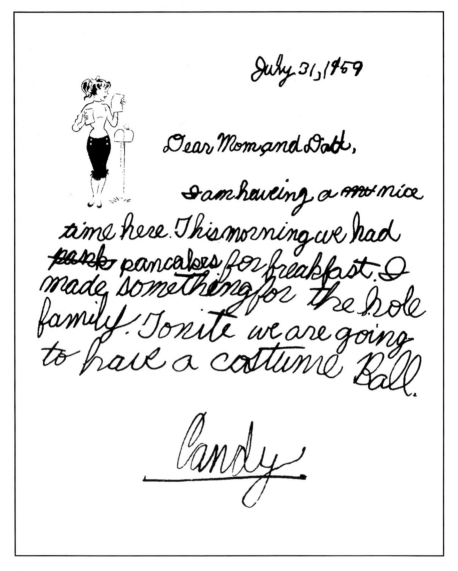

July 31, 1959

Dear Mom and Dad,

I am having a nice time here. This morning we had pancakes for breakfast. I made something for the hole family. Tonite we are going to have a costume Ball.

Candy

Dear Mom 4. *Courtesy of Candi Smith.*

Every summer, the Canandaigua post office had to be a tad busier with letters to and from Camp Onanda. While the pictures on the postcards likely changed through the years, it's almost a sure thing that the messages were pretty much the same.

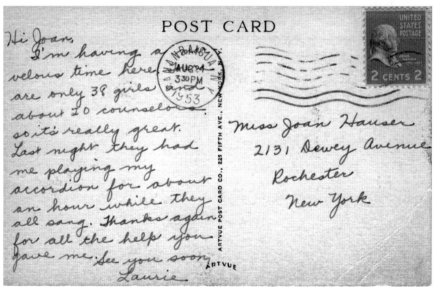

Top: Archery at camp. *Author's collection.*

Bottom: Writing home. *Author's collection.*

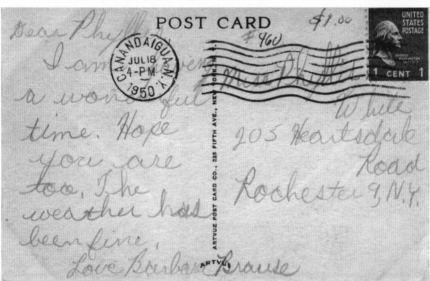

Top: An aerial view of Camp Onanda. *Author's collection.*

Bottom: A message from camp. *Author's collection.*

Obviously, most letters home were brief, likely because they were "required." But what of the memories and impact Onanda had on these girls of summer? When an invitation was sent out to share memories and the impact of Onanda as this book was compiled, the responses were instant.

Right: Tennis lessons. *Author's collection.*

Below: A postcard home from one of the campers. *Author's collection.*

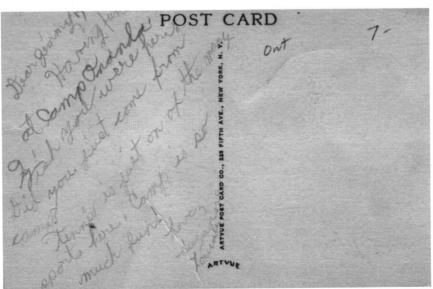

So often Onanda girls shared how camp helped build their confidence and self-awareness or how lifelong friendships were made. Then, too, there were adventures that could only be experienced at summer camp. Even meals were a source of fond memories.

> *Of course, no memory of Onanda is complete without mentioning Zebra Cake. It was so fantastic that I sent my mother to talk to the cook and get the recipe when she picked me up at the end of the camp session. In the end, my mother's Zebra Cake did not come close to Onanda's version.*

A former counselor shared her appreciation for the camp cooks:

> *I don't remember being as hungry at home as I was at camp. Must have been that outdoor work but the kitchen staff was amazing! Never did I leave a meal feeling hungry and Cook Carol, or Millie, I think that was their names, would often give me a cookie or snack on the sly.*

Sometimes campfire snacks were not at all what they sounded like. Here are some misconceptions about snacks shared by Linda:

> *I remember my first campfire at Onanda well. Snacks were offered, and I remember Muff saying that bug juice cups should be put in the can when we had finished. Bug juice! I wasn't about to drink anything made with bugs! Only after a friend asked me why I never had bug juice did I learn that it really had nothing to do with bugs.*

Then there were the memories of "questionable" activities and pranks.

June Cuthbert remembered a promise her counselors kept. Her cabin hadn't found time or good weather to go glen sliding during their session, and the session was nearly over. Her counselors decided the only time they could go would be at night. The cabin had to swear never to talk about it, if they actually agreed to do it. Doing this was so against the rules. If the camp director found out, it would be a very bad situation. The cabin promised not to tell.

> *Around one in the morning, our counselors woke us and we made the dangerous hike down into the glen. We then lined the side of the falls with our flashlights and had a blast. I think the camp director did find out about this, but I don't know how she did.*

A former counselor shared:

Onanda simply gave me a confidence in myself that I had lacked. I learned that teaching should be fun and carried that into my classroom. Every year my class would pull a prank on the principal of the school. One year, one of my fifth graders asked where I learned these things, knowing well of my history of class pranks. I simply smiled and told him that I learned it all at summer camp.

Martha claims she'll never forget when her cabin was in charge of flag raising. Their cabin had practiced their drill a "gazillion" times the day before, but they sure weren't ready for what they found that morning. As they marched up to the flagpole looking smart and official, suddenly, the girl with the folded flag just stopped.

The rest of us sort of bumped into each other and when we looked up at flagpole we all started giggling. There, hanging from the very top of the flagpole, was an oar! Our counselors bailed us out by bringing down the oar so we could put up the flag.

Many a morning something unusual was found atop Camp Onanda's flagpole. Lifejackets, towels or who knows what could disrupt a well-rehearsed raising of the flag. And like so many well-planned events at camp, sometimes they just didn't go as planned. Oddly, but likely not, it was a prank of some sort that disrupted the flow, and it was the prank that was remembered. Laura remembered one of the counselors' pranks on the campers.

One night on Teen Hill, all the cabins were awakened by sound of a siren! Our counselors told us to get shoes on, grab one personal item and follow them to the washhouse. We were really scared, but our counselors just kept saying it was a fire drill.

When we got to the washhouse, Sparks, dressed in a rain slicker and rubber boots, was shouting directions through a megaphone from under a tree laced with toilet paper. No trees were anywhere near the washhouse, so that was beyond strange. There was also a huge metal barrel with flames flying from it by the washhouse.

I think Sparks talked about fire safety, put out the fire and then made us sing a song.

We were then told to go back to our cabins and get some sleep.

The next day, when we started talking about the fire drill and asking our counselors about it, they made like they didn't know what we were talking about. We went straight to Sparks and asked her what it was all about, and she too said didn't know what were talking about.

We campers talked about it and all of us had the strange details of the tree and burning barrel, but all the counselors said we must have dreamed it.

I bet for two days, we thought we had lost our minds until we finally decided we were victims of a prank.

Another former Teen Hill camper remembers a series of pranks between two cabins.

I don't even remember how it all started, but our cabin and Litahni started pulling pranks on each other. It started out with simple things like taking towels and short sheeting beds.

One day, heading to Chule (our cabin) after lunch, we were shocked to find our counselors' beds outside, under the cabin!

One CIT remembers a Sunday evening vesper service:

It was the CITs' job to plan and run the Sunday evening vesper service. Our group did not like the word "sermon," so we chose to prepare a "message." We drew straws to determine who would read this message. I drew the short straw. My fellow CITs assured me that we would all write this document together, and I would just read it on Sunday evening. My heart was not really into this chore, but I knew I could read it if I had to do it. So I practiced reading it through twice before the actual delivery.

After Sunday dinner, the entire camp lined up to walk into the chapel (a really beautiful spot surrounded by trees). We were then informed that the camp director Skip had not yet returned to camp from her day off, and we could not begin without her. We CITs began to worry because the sun was setting, and we had not brought flashlights (and I had not memorized the "message"). The campers did not have flashlights either.

We were finally able to begin the vesper service. We were hurrying through the program before it got completely dark. It was my turn to read the message, and the only light I had was from the candles around the altar. I was reading but not listening to what I was saying when I noticed a tiny blue flame burning across the top of my paper. I was obviously leaning too

Onanda staff, 1972. *Courtesy of the Rochester YWCA.*

Second session campers, 1965. *Courtesy of Nancy Showalter-Clark.*

close to the candle. I chuckled under my breath as I continued to read the words that had no meaning to me while I extinguished the "fire" with my fingertips. As I read, I wondered if anyone else had seen the flames and if this evening could get any worse than it already was. Then it occurred to me that the "message" was written on both sides of the paper and the flame may have destroyed the words on the other side. I got to the bottom of the first page and noticed the sentence continued on the back.

"Oh, no!" I thought. "I don't know what I'm talking about, so I can't fake it. I can't just stop in the middle of the sentence and then look for a new sentence. Or would anyone notice if I did?" Luckily, the words were still there at the top of the next page, and I could mindlessly continue. I was very glad when that vesper service was finished!

Class scheduling was always a challenge. One summer, to meet the requests of campers, a sailing class was added to the after-dinner class schedule. An evening class was generally cooler and calmer, but the calm was not needed for sailing.

Anyone who took sailing lessons during fourth period of the day, after dinner, will remember spending more time tied to the buoy than sailing because there was no evening wind. A sailing camper remembered one of those calm evening classes like this:

On one such evening, we rowed to the sailboat and I, being in the bow of the rowboat, tied us to the buoy. Now sitting in the sailboat, I noticed the rowboat drifting away from us. My knot had slipped. Without missing a beat, our sailing counselor, Truesie, jumped into the water and "rescued" the rowboat. She then climbed back into the sailboat and continued teaching the lesson. After class, everyone on Teen Hill probably heard her squishy footsteps as she walked to the evening campfire program.

There just wasn't anything dull about summer adventures. Every cabin would plan for at least one night sleeping outdoors. The older girls might go off in canoes and sleep at a location somewhere along the lake. Some would hike up into the Primitive Area well beyond the Teen Hill cabins or go to Mel's Double Diamond Ranch or even Ontario County Park near Naples. No matter how well planned these overnights away were, almost every counselor can recall some memorable ones. This was one counselor's memory of an overnight at the ranch:

One session we took an overnight to Mel's. We had younger campers and were riding cabins, so the two cabins had arranged to sleep in the lean-to at the Double Diamond Ranch. The next morning we would ride up Bristol Mountain. We had finally gotten the campers settled in for the night, and we were all in our sleeping bags when raccoons decided to make a visit. I mean, these raccoons were huge! We had left some things out on the picnic table like paper plates and non-food stuff, but they started rummaging through it all.

Salty, the most seasoned counselor, went out and shooed them away and decided that we should hang any and all foodstuffs from a tree. We did this and went back to our sleeping bags.

About five minutes later, Salty announced that something was in her sleeping bag. We all laughed and told her not to scare us any further. She insisted that there was something furry in her bag! Salty leaped up and out of her sleeping bag, grabbed the bag and dashed out of the shelter.

Salty wasn't kidding. We all watched in horror as she flung open her sleeping bag and a mouse scampered out! I don't think any of us slept that night.

While raccoons and mice make for memorable overnights, a couple Trippers groups had notable adventures too. Trippers were made up of older campers. About six girls would go off in the camp station wagon with two counselors. It might be a trip to Mount Marcy, Niagara Falls. It could be a hiking or canoeing trip in the Adirondack Mountains, but it was always different.

One group of Trippers made the local newspaper in LeRoy, New York, after their hiking/camping trip to the Adirondacks. Paps, one of the counselors on this trip, was from LeRoy, and her hometown felt this trip was worthy of sharing. These campers were awakened at night and expected to find a raccoon when the trashcan outside their tent tipped over. When Jan, the other counselor, turned her flashlight in the direction of the noise they found a bear standing on its hind legs. The bear was thoroughly enjoying the discarded coconut pudding and scraps from their evening meal.

Would you forget such adventures?

Teen Hill girls who chose to take riflery classes never forgot that opportunity. One camper shared her disappointment that riflery was discontinued. "I think I grew most after having learned to shoot a rifle. The first time I hit the target impressed upon me the facts that: one, I really could control a gun; two, guns were dangerous only when someone didn't know how to use them correctly; and three, in all life activities, I was responsible for how I handled myself. Thanks, Cap, for these lessons."

Camp Onanda provided every girl a safe and enriching environment that fostered personal growth and respect for others. Thus, it was here that many girls found their voice, their strengths, their direction.

Karen Dowd, who lives far from Onanda now, has always made the effort to attend Camp Onanda reunions. She responded to the call for memories, too.

> *For so many of us, Onanda called us to our own beauty and nurtured and guided us to our own "callings." I, like you and so many others who were privileged to call Onanda "home" for many summers and who understood the gifts of Canandaigua Lake, and who sat in the quiet of a dawn from a "chosen spot" on the hill to watch the sun rise over the ridge, know that without having had the Onanda experience, our lives would have been substantively different and far less rich.*

Sarah Solomon came to Onanda as a first-time camper in the summer of 1969 and kept coming through 1976, going from camper to CIT to junior counselor to counselor. Sarah shared her deep connection to camp and Onanda's impact this way:

> *The friendships I enjoyed with those I worked and played with through the years on staff were wonderful—keeping me buoyed and strong in what I*

Onanda staff, 1966. *Courtesy of Kammie Morrisey.*

was about. Somehow, these magical people at camp coupled with the starry nights, lapping of water, laughing children, goofy jokes and endless music surrounded me with such loving support. It's like they reached down inside of me and found a hiding Sarah. I don't know how else to put it. And I'm quite sure they had no idea what they did for me. People understood me. They valued me.

Sarah's sentiment was echoed by many. Camp Onanda changed shy girls into empowered girls. It created friendships that are binding to this day. It brought out creativity, a love of nature and independence that was carried into their daily lives and has enriched their adult lives. Everyone who shared

Top: Onanda staff, 1974. *Courtesy of Kammie Morrisey.*

Bottom: Reunion day. *Author's collection.*

memories expressed how difficult it was to put their thoughts into words when it came to YWCA Camp Onanda. Still, memories of laughter and music were a constant thread in all the shared memories.

When Camp Onanda gave her call from 1906 to 1987, young women and girls heard that call and answered. They came away from Onanda with an indescribable, new depth of person and memories that would put a sparkle in their eyes always.

Such a legacy!

It comes as no surprise that the girls of summer have often had reunions. At first, they would try to rally every ten years, but now, as summers at Camp Onanda distance themselves, they gather together every five years. While laughter, singing and remembering those summers long ago are constant at these gatherings, sharing of grandchildren, losses and life challenges flow easily as well. There is just some unexplained bond that holds campers and counselors of YWCA Camp Onanda forever together.

There are too many facets to the impact that Camp Onanda has had on lives to adequately relate here, yet it's obvious that the impact was great. As mentioned from the beginning of this sharing, a history is never complete. Parts of any history remain personal, close to the heart, never to be shared but rather meant to be forever cherished deep within.

Listen! Did you hear that? Onanda is calling out to you! Grab a jacket, pack up a picnic and answer her call! Feel the impact for yourself and keep the adventure going!

Resources

The wonderful Albert R. Stone photographs of 1922 scenes at Camp Onanda used in this book, with publication rights secured, are from the Albert R. Stone Negative Collection at the Rochester Museum & Science Center in New York.

Many of the Rochester, New York newspaper articles and all references to the minutes of the YWCA of Rochester were found in the *Young Women's Christian Association of Rochester and Monroe County Collection* at the Rare Books Special Collections & Preservation Department of the University of Rochester in New York. This collection included scrapbooks kept by the YWCA as well as the sited materials.

Other photos and oral or written memories of Camp Onanda and Onanda Park were used with permission.

You may want to check out these websites:
Camp Onanda—www.ywcacamponanda.com
Onanda Park—www.townofcnandaigua.org/parksrec.htm
Ontario County Historical Society—www.ochs.org
Rochester Museum & Science Center—www.rmsc.org
Rare Books and Special Collections at the University of Rochester—www. lib.rochester.edu/rbk
Camp Good Days and Special Times—www.campgooddays.org

Index

About the Author

For well over two decades, Carol Truesdale enjoyed summers with her family on the east side of Canandaigua Lake. For three summers in the late 1960s, she worked as a waterfront counselor at the YWCA's Camp Onanda. A lifetime resident of New York State, State University of New York–Geneseo graduate and retired teacher, Carol pursues her interests in history, music and photography. She is a member of the Ontario County Historical Society and the American Society of Composers, Authors and Publishers (ASCAP) and recently has won recognition for her photography.

Visit us at
www.historypress.net
....

This title is also available as an e-book